Mickey —

you're a joy to work with,
and I know you will
have a lifetime of wonderful
vacations & weekends with
your family. (...hope this book
adds something extra to your
adventures!)

Joan.

9/26/86

Barbara Bailey Kelley is a busy, award-winning writer as well as a mother. She has been published in the acclaimed "The Children's Advocate," and she has participated in local cooperative preschool programs with her two children.

Toni M. Tomacci is Director of the Children's Cultural Arts and Science Workshop in San Jose, California. In addition to lecturing, she has developed an original cultural studies program and has implemented unique hands-on science activities for youngsters, both the fruit of ten years experience as a preschool teacher.

THE
VACATIONS &
WEEKENDS
LEARNING GUIDE
Ideas and Activities to Help Children Learn Throughout the Year

BARBARA BAILEY KELLEY & TONI M. TOMACCI

Illustrations by Marion Ainger

Children's art by Shannon Kelley, Aimee Akaki, Christopher Hayashida, Christopher Newman

A SPECTRUM BOOK
Prentice-Hall, Inc., Englewood Cliffs, New Jersey 07632

Library of Congress Cataloging in Publication Data

Kelley, Barbara Bailey (date).
    The vacations & weekends learning guide.

    "A Spectrum Book."
    Includes bibliographies and index.
      1. Educational games.   2. Recreation.
3. Creative activities and seat work.
I. Tomacci, Toni M. (date).   II. Title.
III. Title: Vacations and weekends learning
guide.
GV1480.K44 1983   371.3'97   82-12355
ISBN 0-13-940130-X
ISBN 0-13-940122-9 (pbk.)

This book is available at a special discount when ordered in large quantities. Contact Prentice-Hall, Inc., General Publishing Division, Special Sales, Englewood Cliffs, N.J. 07632

10 9 8 7 6 5 4 3 2 1

ISBN 0-13-940130-X

ISBN 0-13-940122-9 {PBK.}

Editorial/production supervision
and interior design by Kimberly Mazur
Cover design by Jeannette Jacobs
Manufacturing buyer: Cathie Lenard

The extract from "The Little Turtle" is from *Collected Poems* by Vachel Lindsay. Copyright 1920 by Macmillan Publishing Co., Inc., renewed 1948 by Elizabeth C. Lindsay. The fingerplay hand motions used in "The Turtle Song" are from *Eye Winker, Tom Tinker, Chin Chopper . . . 50 Musical Fingerplays*, by Tom Glazer, Doubleday & Co., New York. © Tom Glazer, used by permission. "I'm Looking Over the Parts of a Flower" is reprinted through the courtesy of JoAnn McElligott Peters. "The Great Thumbless Survival Test" is © 1976 by the Yolla Bolly Press. A Brown Paper School Book.

The poem "Round Is a Pancake" appeared in a reading series in 1966. Its author is Joan Sullivan. We have made every effort to contact Joan Sullivan. The publisher of the reading series in which the poem appears has not been able to locate her at this time, nor have we. The hand motions for this poem are from Sister Betty Shields.

Prentice-Hall International, Inc., London
Prentice-Hall of Australia, Pty. Limited, Sydney
Prentice-Hall Canada Inc., Toronto
Prentice-Hall of India Private Limited, New Delhi
Prentice-Hall of Japan, Inc., Tokyo
Prentice-Hall of Southeast Asia Pte. Ltd., Singapore
Whitehall Books Limited, Wellington, New Zealand
Editora Prentice-Hall do Brasil Ltda., Rio de Janeiro

I dedicate this book to Maria Montessori, whose life as a physician and educator continually touches and uplifts the hearts and minds of children throughout the world.

—T. M. T.

I dedicate this book to those whose inspiration means the most to me: my husband Tom and my daughters Shannon and Colleen.

—B. B. K.

CONTENTS

Contents

PREFACE

The nature of the young child is to wonder. This is the guiding force in the youngster's quest for knowledge, a quest that begins in infancy and that, properly fueled, can last a lifetime.

Those of us who play a part in the lives of young children have a very special obligation: We must feed this inherent sense of wonder until it is so much a part of the child's life that it can never be diminished. The question, of course, is how.

It would be easy to assume that the scope of education—for that is what this quest for knowledge is—could be completely contained within the traditional bounds of the school. Yet the child's desire to know pervades every area of his or her life, whether school is in session or not. Thus, the challenge lies in stimulating and enriching the child above and beyond the classroom curriculum.

The book you now hold in your hands will show you how to meet this challenge.

Contained within these pages is the largest collection ever of easy-to-follow learning activities, written specifically for the adult–child team to participate in and enjoy. Teachers can use this book as a resource for alternative activities to augment the regular curriculum.

Parents will find it a valuable guide to spending educationally enriching time with their children at home. Operators of day care centers can use it to structure a stimulating learning environment with any number of children. Neither special materials nor special training are needed to make this book a success.

The activities are designed to turn otherwise undirected play into constructive, yet effortless, learning experiences which still maintain a strong element of fun. They have been chosen for their ability to actualize the potential of the *whole* child—that is, to expand many of the interests the child may already have, while helping the youngster to develop ones that have yet to be discovered. The activities are open-ended in nature; different phases of each are geared to meet different needs in different children. In short, there is something—no, make that *many* things—for every child in the pages to follow.

But enough about this book. After all, it is nothing more than a tool. What really counts is the time you have to share with the children in your care. Use this time to enhance the special sense of wonder and joy that is the essence of childhood and your reward will far outweigh any effort you put in: The children will grow in intellectual curiosity and knowledge, self-esteem, and self-sufficiency.

And with a combination like that, all things are possible.

THANK YOU

To all those who so freely shared their time and their thoughts with us in the preparation of this book. We gratefully acknowledge the invaluable assistance we received from Mary Kennan, Lisa Femmel, and Kim Mazur of Prentice-Hall, Inc., in writing and refining the manuscript. In addition, Toni M. Tomacci would like to offer special thanks to Joan Ohanneson for her generous and loving support and inspiration.

THE
VACATIONS &
WEEKENDS
LEARNING GUIDE

INTRODUCTION

Perhaps the most sensible way to explain what this book is all about is to tell you how it came to be . . .

One late spring afternoon, a mother stopped by her daughter's Montessori preschool and asked the teacher to suggest some activities to do at home: activities, she explained, that would extend the learning experiences that had taken place during the school year, not to mention chase away the summer blues. The teacher responded with some ideas off the top of her head. The mother wrote them down, then one—I can't remember which—said to the other, "This would make a great book."

Which is exactly what happened. As the book gradually took form, its writers came to realize something else. These activities, which bring the intellectual stimulation of the school environment to the home, also could work in the other direction to bring the nurturing and relaxed atmosphere of the home into the school.

And thus this book came to be what it is: the union of ideas from an educator and a parent on how to nurture, love, stimulate, motivate, encourage, and inspire children, in the home, school, or day care center.

GENERAL GUIDELINES

Before you begin your projects, keep in mind a few guidelines on child development and behavior.

The first guideline relates to *order*. It is important to do these activities—or any others—in a well-ordered way. Children learn by doing; by doing things in an externally ordered way, they will be fostering a sense of internal order that will free them of unnecessary distraction, thereby paving the way for success.

Always be neat. It speeds things up as well as settling things down. Assemble all your materials and tidy up the work area before you begin, then all your attention can be focused on the project at hand.

Organize your time as well. Choose a convenient time for each activity, when all those involved will be fresh. Try to schedule the activity a day ahead, and tell the children in advance. When an activity is planned for a future time or date, the children are much more tolerant about allowing you the time to do what you must. In addition, you can organize your own day so that ample time for the activity is allotted.

In short, organize enough to assure success and accomplishment, but do not confuse order with lack of flexibility. Get to know each individual child's interest levels, needs, and abilities before selecting any activity so that you can choose an appropriate one. Encourage children to develop natural interests at their own pace. The child who spends hours drawing is listening to his or her own inner development timetable, and so should you. You might encourage this child to explore other areas within the scope of this interest, but be sure to keep the youngster supplied in paper, nonetheless. By the same token, let each child do as much of each activity as he or she is capable of doing. Even if a child is not able to do one or more of the steps involved, make sure he or she watches closely. Next time, this child may be able to do the entire activity independently.

With flexibility comes the elimination of gender or grade-level stereotyping. Just as there are no activities in this book that are meant for either males or females (either child or adult), specific age levels are not recommended for the very reason that they can negatively restrict a child. As the adult who knows the children best, it's up to you to choose which activities are right for them at this time. That way, you can still listen to their developmental clocks while increasing their knowledge no matter what their ages.

Children learn by doing, but they also learn by talking about it. Although you don't want to indulge in distracting "chatty" conversation while participating in the activities, do use discussion as much as possible. Ask and invite questions. Use inquiry rather than statement to present facts (for example, "What are some things plants need to stay healthy?" rather than "Plants need . . ."). Never stifle the children's comments. Instead, let group dynamics take over as much as possible; you'll be surprised and pleased at what lengths you'll reach. Be sure to involve everyone in the group in your conversations, directing specific questions to the interests of particular children.

Finally, a word about discipline. For an orderly presentation, you must also have orderly behavior. In most cases, the children's participation and enjoyment will naturally eliminate any behavior problems. However, it is a good idea to establish ground rules at the beginning regarding work areas, special handling of equipment, and cautions with regard to safety and cleaning up. If a child appears restless, give this child a special chore before he or she distracts the others. This added responsibility will channel excess energy and will lead to appropriate behavior. Should a child get out of control, offer a "time-out" where the child is isolated from the group for a short period. This is not punishment per se but a time for the child to regain control while observing the appropriate group behavior as a model. By seeing what he or she is missing, the child will soon be motivated to rejoin the group.

IN PARTICULAR

And now a few tips about using the book itself.

The activities follow a simple and orderly recipe-style format that will be easy for any adult to follow, regardless of his or her previous experience with children. Each activity or field trip is divided into systematic sections that are consistent from chapter to chapter.

Each chapter begins with "An Apple from the Teacher," which provides specific guidelines for maximizing enjoyment and intellectual growth within that subject area. It places the activities within the framework of general child development and describes the benefits of the topic.

Each individual activity and field trip begins with a rationale that describes the scope and special meaning of the activity. Next comes "Setting the Stage," designed to generate and focus the child's interest through a preactivity discussion. This sample dialogue can be read to the child verbatim or it can be used simply as a guideline.

"What You'll Need" follows, with a list of all the necessary materials, in proper order. "How to Do It" spells out, step by step, exactly how the activity is to be done, and "What Else" offers suggestions for follow-up activities to keep the child's interest alive.

The field trips, which come after the activities in each chapter, follow an equally consistent format. "What to Do Before You Go" tells the adult how to arrange the trip and prepare the children for it. "What to Do When You're There" offers general suggestions on how to get the most out of the trip, and "What to Do Afterward" follows up with related thought-provoking discussion and activity.

At the end of each chapter is a list of reading materials for both adult and child that may provide further information and insight into any of the topics introduced in that chapter.

Last, the book's Appendix is a handy tool you can use at a glance to see in which situations, other than the ordinary group, activities in this book can be used.

. . . AND THE RESULT

The goal of childhood is to create an individual self through constructive interaction with the environment. This can be achieved through play. With the help of these activities, you can bring direction to what children normally do to have fun by turning aimless play into *constructive* play.

As the adult participating with the child in these activities, you are contributing to the development of humankind in a very special way: The child is the basic unit of society. By helping him or her to develop full potential, you are directly improving the quality of the world for the next generation.

To interact thus with the young child is an obligation, yet it is also a privilege. If you are a parent (either by "nature" or "for the day"), take your nurturing relationship with the child one step further by guiding and stimulating the child intellectually. If you are a teacher, use these activities at school to bring another element of warmth and relaxation to the classroom.

Above all else, be joyful in what you do. This attitude will be reflected in the child's orderly work pattern and personal contentment. What is more, you will be openly sharing with the child what he or she wants more than anything else—your love and approval.

CHAPTER ONE

ART

AN APPLE FROM THE TEACHER

 Artistic possibilities are as limitless as human possibiiities. With each stroke of creativity, the artist brings into existence some modification of his or her environment. This change may be functional, such as dishing up a new omelette for breakfast. Or it may be purely aesthetic, such as rendering a seascape with some charcoal on paper.

Ideally, each stroke of creativity will give rise to an expression perfectly balanced in design and function. The omelette is garnished with fresh fruit wedges and served at an attractive table; the seascape tells its viewer something of the nature of the sea.

Regardless of their respective media, all artists have this in common: the ability to bring concrete form to an idea. To do this, the artist must have technical skills as well as the mental ability to guide those skills into successful action. Just as we all learn to speak by monosyllabic cooing, artists, craftsmen, and inventors get their start by innocently toying with the various tools they have at their disposal. Leisurely hours with a paint set may lead to great discoveries in color, and endless combinations of building blocks may plant the seed for innovative architecture.

Architect Frank Lloyd Wright, for example, vividly recalls playing with geometric Froebel building blocks as a child. Even a brief encounter with his work will show the influence of those innocent blocks on this great mind.

This chapter provides theoretical information along with many skill-in-action activities. Remember as you work with your child that practice refines a skill and orderly practice maximizes the process. Here are some guidelines to keep in mind while organizing your projects:

Store materials in a neat and efficient way. Tackle boxes are sturdy and have lots of nifty little spaces to turn an array of crayons, pencils, templates, and scissors into a media library neatly awaiting its next patron. Other useful storage containers are cans or jars with decorative labels. Napkin holders can be used to store small pieces of paper, and standard-sized desk trays do the same for larger pieces.

Professional artists make many "cartoons" or beginning sketches before finally producing the finished masterpiece. So, too, most children will experiment with different possibilities before producing one that is "just right." We certainly don't want to curtail this process by giving lectures about wasting paper with repetitious scribbling, yet we want to make the best use of our resources. This can be dealt with in two ways: First, take advantage of free or very cheap paper from architects (blueprints), printers, and the ever-present computers. Second, after you've seen the fiftieth identical 2-by-2-inch flower scrawled on an 8½-by-11-inch sheet, introduce some open-ended assignments, such as "Fill this page with as many colors (or triangles, or curved shapes, or things you can eat) as possible." Or perhaps you might pencil in territories for each object to be drawn in. These guidelines are fertile ground for the exploration of new possibilities.

In short, you can see that fifty identical flowers waste more than paper. *The Anti-Coloring Book* by Susan Striker and Edward Kimmel creatively launches children into the open-ended process.

What to do with the masterpieces once they are completed can be quite a dilemma. You know that each artistic endeavor is an outward expression of the child's inner self, so how could you possibly throw away something of this stature? But refrigerators and bulletin boards can only hold so much. What can best respect both the child and the work? Here are a few suggestions:

1. Keep artwork in a box or folder from which you may choose featured pieces to be displayed on bulletin boards or behind a matboard frame.
2. Children can use small paper designs for stationery and larger ones for wrapping paper.

3. A parent can take a collection of favorite designs to a printer and have them bound. This makes a great Christmas gift for adoring grandparents, and handily takes care of 100 or more drawings. Growth in style and skill can be nicely shown in a collection made over a period of time.

A brief word about coloring books. Children love them, and they offer great exercises in perceptual and fine motor skills. They really shouldn't be thought of as stifling creativity. Instead, they lay the groundwork for furthering it. Coloring is also a settling activity after a busy day. Finally, once children have explored coloring possibilities on their own, some open-ended suggestions are in order, such as "Design your ideal house," or "Make a design using shapes, such as circles, squares, and triangles."

Constructive praise is the best reinforcement for children's work. Your opinion is valued, so naturally children will feel good when you like their work. But how much more accomplished the youngsters will feel when you cite specific things they have done. For example, "Christopher, you drew that person with twenty-seven body parts!" or "Shannon, your house has two gables with storm windows." This way, the children will gain much more than your approval. They will grow in self-esteem.

PENS, PAPERS, YARN, MAGAZINES, AND SHAVING CREAM— AND ANYTHING ELSE THAT MAKES A PICTURE

Challenge any kid you know to make a picture without the traditional tools of the trade and, chances are, you'll have one stymied child on your hands. The youngster is undoubtedly so accustomed to drawing with crayons or marking pens on paper that other ways to create have yet to be thought of.

In the following activity, children learn to use a whole spectrum of everyday objects for creative purposes. The children get practice in different fine motor skills as well as in several art techniques. They increase their experience with an awareness of color, design, and texture.

Yet this entire group of activities is a means to an end rather than an end in itself: The newness of these techniques serves to enliven the artistic pastime. The child ends up spending time more productively on each project. What's more, using new ways to create is in itself an open-ended and creative activity. Each new medium sparks the child's desire to explore other possibilities for design on a unique and independent basis.

Invite the boys and girls to explore new and unusual ways to make pictures:

> If you wanted to draw a picture, what would you use? A box of crayons? Paper? Pencils? How about shaving cream? Or Q-tips?
>
> In the same way that you can draw anything you can imagine, you can also draw *with* just about anything you can imagine. Here are some examples.

Dip Dots

WHAT YOU'LL NEED

1. Water
2. Food coloring
3. A small container for each color
4. Q-tips
5. Paper—any shape, color, size, or texture

HOW TO DO IT

1. Mix ¼ cup of water with about 10 drops of food coloring in each container.
2. Use the Q-tips to apply the color to the paper by dotting, rolling, or streaking it across the paper.
3. Color-mix by dipping the Q-tips in two colors before applying the color to the paper.

Shaving Cream Pictures

WHAT YOU'LL NEED

1. A waterproof table top
2. Newspapers or plastic tarpaulin
3. Shaving cream
4. Food coloring
5. Paper
6. Sponge

HOW TO DO IT

1. Spread newspaper or tarpaulin under the worktable to protect the floor.
2. Squirt a small amount of shaving cream onto the table top.
3. Sprinkle a few drops of food coloring onto the shaving cream.
4. Mix the color into the shaving cream and spread it over the table until it forms a thin film. (Hands are the best mixing tools.)

5. Finger-paint a design into the film.
6. Place a sheet of paper on top of the design and press down on it with clean, dry hands.
7. Carefully lift up the paper and let it dry.
8. Clean up with sponge and warm water.

Rubbings

WHAT YOU'LL NEED
1. Paper, the thinner the better
2. Crayons, with the paper removed

HOW TO DO IT
1. Place the paper over anything with an interesting texture, such as a tree, linoleum floor, wall, or sidewalk. Or gather several small items, such as a leaf, some lace, and a twig, and arrange them in an interesting design on a hard, flat surface.
2. Rub the side of the crayon all over the paper.

Hot Crayons

WHAT YOU'LL NEED
1. Electric warming tray
2. Aluminum foil
3. Paper
4. Small sponge
5. Crayons

HOW TO DO IT
1. Cover the tray with foil.
2. Turn the tray onto the lowest setting.
3. Place the paper on the tray. (Children can use sponges to hold their papers in place.)
4. Color on the paper. Caution the children to go slowly so that each crayon stroke will melt, but not so slowly that the melted crayon forms a puddle.
5. Have each child hold up the finished creation to a light source and compare it to regular crayon drawings.
6. Try this technique in other ways:
   • Use only crayons that are different shades of the same color.
   • Color designs within the boundaries of the squares on a sheet of graph paper.
   • Trace and combine the basic shapes on engineering or artist's templates.

Wet Chalk Drawing

1. Colored chalk
2. A small bowl of water
3. Paper or paper towels

HOW TO DO IT
1. Dip the chalk in the water.
2. Draw. The chalk tip must stay wet.

Magazine Montage

WHAT YOU'LL NEED
1. Old magazines
2. Scissors
3. Paper
4. Paste
5. Marking pens

HOW TO DO IT
1. Let each child choose a subject for the montage. Here are a few examples: things to eat, things to play with, favorite things, or people showing similar emotions. Another fun idea is to put cut out pictures together in a new way to make something whimsical, such as a dog driving a car or an airplane parked in a driveway.
2. Search through magazines to find pictures to fit the theme. Cut them out.
3. Paste the pictures onto the paper in an attractive design.
4. Add any special details the montage might need with a marking pen.

What Else

Of course, there are dozens of other ways to create pictures, like crayon-etching, glueing yarn to paper, or making "combs" out of cardboard to form designs in wet sand. But it may be time to just turn the children's imaginations loose and let them do the thinking. Chances are, the budding artists will come up with ways to make pictures that you've never even dreamed of. The children can even make pictures of a more lasting nature by embroidering an original design on a piece of burlap, a small towel, or even an article of clothing.

You might also want to fill a box with supplies such as scraps of yarn, colored paper, fabric, and old magazines, in addition to paper, scissors, paste, and glue. On rainy days (or other times when morale is on the wane), let each child dig into the box for treasures with which to create a masterpiece.

And when you want a change of pace from picture making, have the children take the pictures they made that day, then search for objects that match the design.

BENDING LIGHT

Has there ever been a child who has not delighted in water play—especially on hot, sunny days? "Bending Light" turns fun with a hose into a scientific learning experience that provides happy youngsters with even more insight into the spectral composition of color.

The following activity is designed to increase children's sense of wonder at the beauty inherent in their universe. As the girls and boys re-create the magic of the rainbow right in their play yard, their scientific curiosity will be stimulated. Not only will the children gain more knowledge about color—knowledge that will add to their appreciation of it—but their interest in further experimentation with light and color will be heightened.

This activity offers a variety of opportunities for productive outdoor waterplay during the hot summer months, especially when the children are feeling high-spirited. Just turn on the water and let imaginations run free. It's sure to increase *your* sense of wonder at the beauty inherent in the child.

SETTING THE STAGE

Invite each child to look at light in a "new light":

On a bright and sunny day, go outside and take a good look at what you see. There are lots of things all around you, each having its own size, shape, and color.

Now, what is between you and each of the objects you are looking at?

You know there is air, otherwise you wouldn't be able to breathe to stay alive and look around. And since you are able to see anything at all, you know there has to be light.

We don't usually think of seeing light itself. We just see light shining *on* something. That's the way we experience light most of the time. This time, let's try something different.

WHAT YOU'LL NEED
1. A garden hose and faucet
2. Crayons
3. White paper

HOW TO DO IT
1. Hook the hose up to a faucet near an open and sunny area (preferably one that would enjoy some extra moisture).

2. Turn on the water, holding your thumb over the end of the hose so that you can make a wide spray in front of you.
3. Have the children look carefully at what is coming out of the hose. Ask them what they see besides water, where the spray intercepts a beam of sunlight.
4. Ask the children to look closely for the rainbow. Talk about all the different colors that are visible. Let each child draw what he or she sees. Change the position of the spray of water several times. Ask the children if they notice any consistency in the order of the colors from one rainbow to the next. Point out that primary colors always come first, with secondary colors sandwiched in between. (This may inspire the children to experiment with color later on by mixing red-, yellow- or blue-colored water, ice cubes, or tissue paper.)

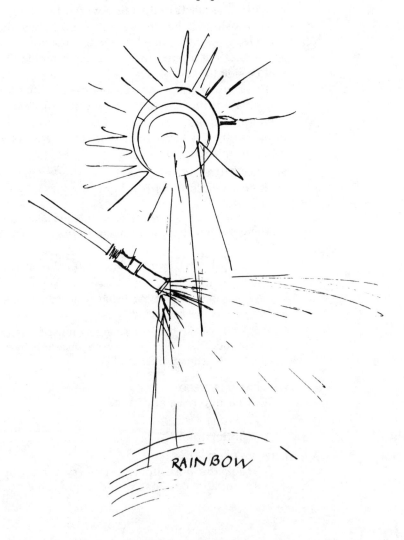

RAINBOW

What Else

When it's time to turn off the water, you might want to continue the discussion inside. Relate the activity to this important (and beautiful) scientific principle: When light passes through a space with clear sides, like a drop of water, it bends. When light bends, it no longer moves at the same speed. Some parts of the light move faster than others. The color of light changes depending on how fast or slowly it is moving; when it passes through a drop of water, we see many different colors because the light is moving at many different speeds. If you happen to have a prism, some cut glass, or even a diamond ring at your disposal, use one of these props to further illustrate the principle.

You can also offer further suggestions for experimentation, such as: "Can you make a rainbow with a hose on a cloudy day? At all times of the day? And what about places where sunlight is blocked?"

Finally, to turn "Bending Light" into a delightfully aesthetic and imaginative exercise, present the young artists with a few hypothetical subjects for related artwork. To get their imagination going, ask them to draw a picture of how the play yard might look from *inside* the rainbow!

HOW TO GET GREEN SOCKS
FROM MORNING GLORIES

The young child is a naturally resourceful creature. (Just look at how rapidly a single-minded youngster can rearrange the playroom in the name of playing house.) Children love asking questions and learning about how things came into being.

On a practical level, they get a thrill from making anything "from scratch."

One way to foster this resourceful spirit is to allow the child to discover and experiment with the way things were made when the only conveniences were those supplied by nature. In the following activity, you and the children can share a trip back to the days of hand-loomed, hand-dyed cloth—while giving them yet another exercise in color awareness. The children are sure to enjoy the experience of doing something themselves that is normally done in the anonymity of the factory. They are sure to gain an appreciation of our American heritage from this brief introduction to pioneer civilization.

And they are likely to become more aware of color in their environment. This may result in a greater scrutiny of the colors in nature, or it may result in a greater scrutiny of the colors in the clothes closet.

In short, this activity may well mark the end of those unique color combinations that are the emblem of children who dress themselves!

SETTING THE STAGE

Invite the children to activate their spirit of resourcefulness while awakening their sense of color:

In the early days of America, there were no clothing stores. There weren't even any fabric stores.

The early settlers had to make all their own clothes. Not only that, they even had to weave the cloth that their clothes were made from!

They wove the fabric from wool or cotton. The problem was, everything ended up a dull, grayish-white color.

So what do you suppose these early Americans did? Do you think all their clothes were the same dull color?

These people liked pretty colors just as much as you do. So they dyed their yarns and fabrics different colors with the flowers, leaves, and bark that grew around them.

You can do it too.

WHAT YOU'LL NEED
1. Undyed yarn, fabric, or an article of clothing that is made of natural fibers
2. Sink
3. 2 large pots
4. Powdered alum
5. Water
6. Stove
7. Strainer
8. Several handfuls of one of the following:

Plant	*Dye color*
Morning glory blossoms	green
Spinach	green
Cherries	red
Red onion skins	red
Tomato vines	reddish-brown
Almonds (nuts and shells)	brown
English walnuts	brown
Apple tree bark	dark yellow
Dandelion blossoms	light yellow
Marigold flowers	yellow
Yellow onion skins	yellow
Calendula flowers	gold
Eucalyptus leaves	orange
Pine cones	orange

SPINACH!?
Let's dye some socks!

Nasturtium flowers	peach
Crabapples	pink
Grapes	purple
Privet berries	blue

Have the children experiment with the amount to use. Some dyes require more plant matter than the others and are stronger during different seasons.

HOW TO DO IT

1. Wash the article to be dyed. (We'll call it socks from here on.)

*2. Mix 2 tablespoons of alum and 1 gallon of hot water in a large pot. This will make a *mordant,* which is a soaking solution that helps the fibers retain the dye. (Although many mordants are dangerous chemicals, powdered alum is quite safe.)

*3. Put the socks into the mordant. Let them soak 1 hour.

*4. Prepare the dyebath by adding the chosen leaves, flowers, or bark to 1 gallon of boiling water in the second big pot. Keep

*Because of the obvious hazard presented by the hot and boiling water, and because some dyes can be toxic, either do these portions of the activity yourself or restrict them to older children.

adding until the water turns a vibrant color that is agreeable to the child.

5. Simmer the dyebath 1 hour.
*6. Use the strainer to remove the plant matter from the dyebath.
7. Remove the socks from the mordant and wring them out.
*8. Put the socks into the dyebath. Let them simmer 1 hour. (Make note of the color of the dyebath.)
*9. Remove the socks from the dye with the strainer. Rinse them with warm water until the rinsing water runs clear. (How does the color of the socks compare with the color of the dye bath?)

What Else

During the waiting periods of this activity, you might want to do a comparison of pioneer life to contemporary life. Discuss the things the early settlers had to do for themselves in order to survive. Ask the children to name some of the modern conveniences we tend to take for granted, then ask them how they might do without them.

You can also try these color (or lack of color) experiments to teach the children its value in our everday lives: Have the children draw pictures in which everything is gray. If it is practical, hide everything in the playroom that is a pretty color (except for the furniture, rug, and curtains). Have each child plan a meal of foods that are all the same color. Or ask the children to all wear the same color the next day.

Children who want to learn more about natural dyes might want to experiment on their own. Send them out on a nature walk to collect some blossoms, leaves, or berries. Ask them to guess what color dyes these will make. Then let them use these dyes to see how close their guess came. Read *Contemporary Batik and Tie-Dye* by Dona Z. Meilach and *Tie-Dye* by Sara Nea to give the children some creative ideas on what to do with the dyes once they've made them. And to get a free booklet on using the batik method at home, send a postcard to AEB, Box 307, Coventry CT 06238. Ask for "The Art of Easy Batik."

HOW FAR IS NEAR?
EXPERIMENTS IN PERSPECTIVE

One of the most beautiful things about children is their natural curiosity. One way to nurture it is to provide them with ever-increasing means for discovery.

Teaching youngsters about perspective is one way to put more of the secrets of the universe within their grasp because it gives the children a clearer understanding of their environment. What child has not asked, at one time or another, "If the moon is so big, why does it look so small?" Knowledge of perspective gives even the most inquisitive youngster some answers.

Knowledge of perspective can also increase children's visual awareness by making everyday observation more fun and interesting. On a practical level, perspective techniques can increase their graphic creativity and skill at accurate illustration, which, in turn, will make them feel better about their work.

In short, teaching a child perspective can be one way to lick the "I can't make it look right" blues.

SETTING THE STAGE

Invite the children to explore a new drawing technique as a way to understand why small things sometimes look big and why big things sometimes look small:

Have you ever visited an airport? Perhaps you have even been in an airplane yourself. If you have, you know how very big airplanes are.

They are so big, in fact, that lots of people bigger than yourself can fit in one.

Now—if an airplane is so gigantic when you see it on the ground, why does that same airplane look as small as an ant when you see it in the sky?

The answer is *perspective*. Perspective refers to why things seem to change in size depending on how close or far away they are.

Perspective is also a way of drawing that you can use in your own artwork when you want to show that something is close up or far away.

WHAT YOU'LL NEED
1. Paper
2. Pens or pencils

HOW TO DO IT
1. Go outside and look at the house or building closest to you. Then turn around and look at a house or building across the street that you know is similar in size to the first building. Ask each child which one *seems* to be smallest?
2. Explain this technique of perspective: Objects that are farther away look smaller than they really are. Have the children draw a picture using this technique.
3. Stand between the children and the building closest to you. Ask the children how they know that you are closer to them than the building is. Point out that they can see all of you but only part of the building, because you are blocking the view.
4. Explain principle number two: Objects that are closer to you block your view of objects that are behind them. Have the children use this technique in a drawing.

5. Stand in front of the children. Tell them to look carefully at your face. Then back away from the group until you are at least 30 to 40 feet away. Ask each child to tell if you are smiling or frowning.
6. Explain this final principle: You can see more detail in objects that are close than in objects that are far away. Have the children draw a picture using this technique.

What Else

Once the children begin to understand the techniques of perspective, they can put them to practical use to create a fine picture of the landscape, the play yard, or even the view from the front window.

Here is another way to give an eager child practice. Cut out a magazine picture that shows one or more elements of perspective. Paste it on the bottom of a piece of paper. Have the child pick out the

objects that are the biggest or most detailed. Have the child figure out which objects go in front of the others in the picture, then copy the picture on the top half of the page.

You might want to wrap up the activity with a theoretical discussion of perspective. Ask the children such questions as "How can you tell which car is closest to you when you are driving on the highway?" or "When you're standing in a forest, how can you tell which trees are farthest away?"

Finally, explore the magic of perspective in *From Afar It Is an Island* by Bruno Munari.

MAKE YOUR OWN PUZZLE

While a child's pudgy little fingers struggle with the pieces of a picture puzzle, all sorts of wonderful things are happening within his or her mind. As the child becomes cognizant of the relationship of the parts to the whole, concrete experience can be translated into the understanding of abstract concepts. (For instance, it will become clear that four triangles are still four triangles even when they are assembled to make one larger triangle.) The youngster develops perceptual skills and sharpens fine motor skills at the same time. Each time a puzzle is successfully completed, the child's self-confidence grows by leaps and bounds.

In the following activity, you can take the benefits of doing puzzles one step further by reversing the process—that is, teaching the children to construct a puzzle from a picture.

This activity gives girls and boys further practice in abstraction and problem solving. They gain insight into the makeup of a favorite toy, which in turn may inspire further creativity by giving them confidence in their own planning and technical ability.

What's more, by constructing their own puzzles, the children learn self-sufficiency: Just because something doesn't exist doesn't mean that they can't bring it into being. They discover that they can add another useful skill to their repertoire, and each child has yet another opportunity to proclaim with pride: "Look! I made this all by myself!"

SETTING THE STAGE

Invite each child to begin the project by mentally envisioning the construction of the puzzle:

> Don't you like to play with picture puzzles? Which do you like best? Taking them apart or putting them back together?

> Can you think how you might make a picture puzzle? What do you suppose comes first? The picture or the pieces?

WHAT YOU'LL NEED
1. White glue or paste
2. Cardboard
3. A picture, either cut from a magazine or a child's own work
4. Rolling pin
5. Scissors
6. Pencil
7. Envelope

HOW TO DO IT
1. Glue the picture to the cardboard.
2. Roll it with the rolling pin to smooth out the wrinkles.
3. Trim the sides.
4. Let it dry.
5. Decide how many pieces the puzzle should have.
6. Outline the correct number of pieces on the back with a pencil. They can be any shape or size.
7. Cut the pieces out.
8. Store the pieces in an envelope.

What Else

If more than one child is making a puzzle, let the children trade. They can even race to see who can put another child's together fastest.

Older children can mount their pictures on railroad board or thin plywood, then cut out the pieces with a mat knife or jigsaw. These long-lasting puzzles make excellent gifts for younger brothers or sisters.

As an additional exercise in perception, children can make a two-sided puzzle. Simply mount and cut out a side-view of a dog, for example. Turn the board over and mount a picture of the dog's *other* side. Cut it into pieces as before.

And here's a way to make six puzzles at once while exposing a child to the mathematical properties of cubes. Arrange nine uniformly sized blocks into a tight square. Trim six pictures so that each is the same size as the square. Then cut each picture into nine pieces, each piece the same size as an individual block. Glue one piece of each picture to one side of each block. (Each block is a six-sided cube. By gluing one segment of a picture to each side of each block, you are constructing six separate puzzles.)

Finally, you can directly combine puzzle making with other areas of interest. The future cartographer can make a puzzle from a map. And the beginning reader will delight in making simple puzzles out of words or sentences printed on strips of cardboard.

WHERE THE OTHER ARTISTS
HANG THEIR WORK:
A TRIP TO THE ART MUSEUM

Children may not know much about art, but they know what they like! What better way to begin a lifetime of art appreciation.

Taking young children to the art museum is a valuable way to spend an afternoon (or morning), for many reasons. First, the trip exposes the children to many new artistic possibilities and expands their awareness of them. Even the briefest glance at a piece of art will make an impression on any child and will serve as an inspiration for future endeavors.

Viewing a painting a little while longer can be the catalyst for an open-ended discussion of color, style, and technique.

Second, a trip to the art museum will give the children an opportunity to experience art on a different level. They can enjoy it as a pleasurable visual experience as well as a process-oriented activity.

And finally, by seeing the many works of art on display and the great respect paid them, the children learn that the creation of art is an occupation to be treated with dignity. And because they too are artists, their creative activity is also to be treated with dignity. In short, the children come to view their own artwork with newfound respect. A Picasso-to-be might even be moved to have a "showing" of his own.

A stop at the museum bookstore before the bus ride home can also be a productive experience. Children can usually select an excellent print or book all by themselves. This purchase, combined with the trip itself, will serve as a continuing source of knowledge and inspiration for weeks to come.

SETTING THE STAGE

Invite the children to discover that art can be experienced in many different ways so that they will come to see themselves as artists:

> When we create, we call it *art*. People who create art are called *artists*. Now that *you* have become an artist, you might enjoy looking at other artists' work.
>
> Art can be enjoyed in so many ways! You may enjoy a picture because it's pretty. You may like it because it tells you about something you are especially interested in, like summers at the North Pole.
>
> You can find art just about anyplace, but one place where you're sure to find a lot of art is the art museum.

WHAT TO DO BEFORE YOU GO

1. Find out about the art that is on display at the museum you plan to visit. Is there a special showing? Are there watercolors? Sculpture? How old is the artwork?
2. Show the children books that relate to the artwork on display. Talk about what you'll see.
3. Have each child bring unlined paper and colored pencils or fine-tipped felt pens.
4. Also, make sure that each child has a little extra money for admission charges, if applicable, and for treasures from the gift shop.
5. Review some basic "museum etiquette" and be on your way!

WHAT TO DO WHILE YOU'RE THERE

1. Let the children wander! Since there is so much to see and enjoy, it's best to let them go off in whatever directions seems most

interesting to them. (Just make sure they keep you apprised of their whereabouts.)

2. Encourage the children to stop in front of anything they find especially interesting, take a good look at it, and think about it. You might ask them such questions as "What do you see?" "Why do you think the artist did whatever he or she did?" "How was the artwork created?" "What does it make you think of?" "How does it make you feel?"

3. Turn a trip to the art museum into a treasure hunt by seeking the art that is the funniest, the most colorful, has the most people in it, and so forth.

4. To learn more about the artwork on display, ask a docent to show you around.

5. If there's time, let each child choose a piece of art to sit before and draw.

WHAT TO DO AFTERWARD

1. Discuss the new ways of creating art each child discovered. Try out some of these techniques.

2. Children can make their own art museums at home to display favorite artwork by hanging some corkboard on the wall or by painting the outside of a cardboard box to look like a wall in a museum.

3. Plan another visit to the museum to discover new things you may have missed the first time around.

4. Read through *Looking at Paintings* by Frances Kennet and Terry Meashem to reinforce the new art concepts the children learned about and to prepare for the next visit to the museum.

ART IN ARCHITECTURE

The idea that in architecture, as in nature, beauty resides in function rather than symbolic decoration was first suggested in America little over a century ago. Since then, "form follows function" has been a guiding principle in architectural design throughout our country.

This principle, in fact, may well be the simplest and most effective way to introduce children to the wonders of architecture. That, and a slow stroll around a block of different and beautiful buildings on a warm, summery day.

Helping children to find the reasons behind the special facades, roofs, or windows of the buildings they see will give them an introductory insight into why buildings look the way they do. Thus equipped, the children will begin to notice architecture more and to enjoy and appreciate it. As the youngsters begin "listening to" as well as looking at buildings, they will come that much closer to unraveling the mystery of how houses come to be.

Perhaps this introduction to "art that you can live or work in" will result in the emergence of a Frank Lloyd Wright in your midst. Perhaps not. You can be sure, however, that this enjoyable field trip will make future play with such toys as blocks or building kits more logical, orderly, and purposeful—attributes that will happily carry over into other areas of each child's work.

SETTING THE STAGE

Invite each child to explore a relationship with buildings as a new art form and to listen to what they have to say:

Do you know that there is a different kind of art museum right outside your front door?

There is. It is your own neighborhood. And what do you suppose is on display?

Buildings. They can be old ones or new ones, small houses or large apartment buildings. They can be made of anything from brick to glass to wood. And they are all works of art, because they display the creativity of the person who built them.

Beautiful buildings are built in a balanced way, so that every part of the building has enough support to keep it from falling down.

And beautiful buildings are *functional*. This means that every part of the building serves some purpose for the people who live or work inside.

Buildings become special when they have their own character, when they reflect the personalities of the people who live or work inside them. They also become special when they fit into the style of their surroundings.

I'm sure you think your house or apartment building is the prettiest in the world. Would you like to see some others that are *almost* as special?

WHAT TO DO BEFORE YOU GO

1. Have each child take a good, close look at his or her house or apartment building, and answer these questions about it: "What does it look like?" "Is it tall or short?" "How many floors does it have? What kind of windows?" "Are there straight or curved lines in the building's design?" "Why do you suppose the building was built the way it was?" "Does the building have any special details? What are these for?" "Is there anything about the building that tells you something about the people who live inside?"

2. Have each child draw a picture of this building that includes everything previously noticed about it.

3. Decide on another neighborhood to visit where the buildings will be substantially different from the ones the children are familiar with.

WHAT TO DO WHILE YOU'RE THERE

1. Bring paper and pencils.
2. Invite the children to look carefully at each building and answer these questions about it: "Is it tall or short? Wide or skinny?" "What kind of materials is it built from?" "Does the building have any special details?"
3. Have the children try to guess the function of the building from the way it looks: "What is the reason for each of the details?" "What do you suppose the people are like that live or work inside?"
4. Ask the children to compare the building to their own homes.
5. Let each child draw a picture of a favorite building.

WHAT DO DO AFTERWARD

1. Let the children try to build the buildings they drew out of blocks or a building set. Point out which parts of the building get built first.
2. Have each child draw a picture of a house that would be fun to live in. What would make it so much fun? Where would the child's room be? This book will enhance the process: *Draw 50 Buildings and Other Structures* by Lee J. Ames.
3. Build *this* house out of blocks or a building set.
4. Cut pictures of special buildings out of magazines and paste them into a scrapbook.

5. Find out where new construction is going on in your town. If possible, take the children there to watch the builders at work. If you can, arrange to drive past at regular intervals to watch the progress.
6. Older children will enjoy discussing how they feel when they see or enter a building: Certain architectural features, such as a set of 15-foot-high double doors, let people into buildings the same way a single 7-foot door might. But how you *feel* when you walk through the doors makes the difference. Large doors on a court-house, for example, might make you feel that you are walking into a very important place. This is yet another aspect of the "form follows function" concept.

BOOKS FOR CONTINUING DISCOVERY

Books for Adults

ADROSKO, RITA. *Natural Dyes and Home Dyeing.* New York: Dover, 1971.

AMES, LEE J. *Draw 50 Buildings and Other Structures.* New York: Double-day, 1980.

FIAROTTA, PHYLLIS. *Snips and Snails and Walnut Whales.* New York: Workman Publishing, 1975.

JENKINS, PEGGY DAVISON. *Art for the Fun of It.* Englewood Cliffs, N.J.: Prentice-Hall, 1980.

KENNET, FRANCES, and TERRY MEASHEM. *Looking at Paintings.* New York: Van Nostrand Reinhold, 1978.

MEILACH, DONA Z. *Contemporary Batik and Tie Dye.* New York: Crown Publishers, 1973.

NEA, SARA. *Tie-Dye.* New York: Van Nostrand Reinhold, 1969.

TABER, GLADYS. *Flower Arranging.* New York: Holt, Rinehart & Winston, 1969.

WIRTENBERG, PATRICIA Z. *All Around the House Art and Craft Book.* Boston: Houghton Mifflin, 1968.

WOOD, ANNETTE. *Teaching Art and Crafts in Elementary School.* En-glewood Cliffs, N.J.: Prentice-Hall, 1981.

Books for Children

HOLIDAY, ENSOR. *Altair Design Series.* New York: Pantheon Books, 1978.

LIONNI, LEO. *A Little Yellow, a Little Blue.* New York: Astor-Honor, 1959.

MAC AGY, DOUGLAS and ELIZABETH. *Going for a Walk with a Line.* New York: Doubleday, 1959.

Munari, Bruno. *From Afar It Is an Island.* New York: World Publishing, 1972.

Pinkwater, Daniel Manus. *The Big Orange Splot.* New York: Scholastic Book Service, 1977.

Reiss, John. *Colors.* New York: Bradbury Press, 1969.

Striker, Susan, and Edward Kimmel. *The Anti-Coloring Book.* New York: Holt, Rinehart & Winston, 1978.

Wyler, Rose, and Gerald Ames. *Secrets in Stones.* New York: Four Winds, 1971.

Zacharias, Thomas. *But Where Is the Green Parrot?* New York: Delacorte, 1968.

CHAPTER TWO

FOOD

AN APPLE FROM THE TEACHER

Food! What a glorious topic! No matter what special interests children develop throughout their lives, food will always be a part of their daily experience.

We eat for a lot of reasons (some of which are better than others!). Eating is something fun to do when friends get together. We eat to treat ourselves when something nice happens. And we eat when something not-so-nice happens. Regardless of what our immediate reasons for eating are, one thing remains constant: Our bodies need proper nutrition to stay healthy.

Protein is what our bodies are made of and sugar (not necessarily the kind that comes with a candy bar) is what makes it go. It's that simple. The more we know about the food we eat, the better care we will be able to give to our bodies.

This chapter offers a wide range of food activities that will give your child an increased awareness of where food comes from ("Grow it," "Choose It") and what to do with it ("Cook It," "Serve It," "Store It").

Each activity introduces the child to something that might be brand new ("Sprouting Seeds and Beans"). Or it might be a new twist to something we all take for granted ("Finger Foods"). What is most important here is that you will be sharing new possibilities with foods that are well balanced in variety as well as nutrition.

Studies show that when they are offered meals featuring the four food groups three times a day for seven to ten days, small babies will naturally select the foods that make up a balanced diet. This happens spontaneously; it is the net result of being offered a balanced menu at each meal, even though at any given time the baby may eat a lot of one kind of food and ignore others. The moral of this is "Trust the child to choose what is best." Adults need only offer intelligent alternatives from which to choose. For instance, one would not ask a four-year-old, "What do you want for lunch?" Nor would you say, "Would you like a soda or chewing gum for lunch?" The infinite choices in the first example are as useless as the narrow and inappropriate choices of the second. A good question for our hungry four-year-old would be, "Would you like a sandwich or leftovers from last night's dinner for lunch?" or "Would you like milk or juice to drink? And for dessert, there's fruit or ice cream."

When children are actively involved in selecting and preparing the food they eat, they are more likely to become intelligent menu planners rather than passive consumers who either accept or reject what is placed before them. While introducing the child to more enjoyable and smart ways to eat, approach each activity as you would a fun craft project. For instance, orderliness in your work area makes things less confusing. However, what cup of flour has ever *entirely* landed in the mixing bowl? In other words, you must expect—and live with—a few spills and, perhaps, less-than-perfectly-sliced fruit for your salad. You can maximize your efforts toward the finished product, however, by giving your child utensils that are child-sized whenever possible. For example, while it may take a little longer, it will be much easier for someone with a tiny and unskilled hand to measure out flour with a soupspoon rather than a measuring spoon. And whether or not the finished product is ready for the bake-off at the State Fair, the child's own special (and, quite often, tasty) creation deserves service in real dishes. How appropriate to serve your teddy-bear-shaped finger sandwiches on a child's favorite plate instead of balancing them on a paper towel or napkin.

As was said at the outset, this chapter offers ways in which you and the children in your care may share a new approach to our daily bread, while bolstering each child's self-confidence and sparking new interests and skills. This chapter is also a great way to insure that boys see cooking as an integral part of their lives, too. However, as you work with food that is easily taken for granted, always be open to new ways to do old things and to capitalize on the child's natural sense of wonder. What is the magic of boiling water that lets it turn a soft egg hard or hard macaroni soft?

And how did *you* discover that French Fries were made from potatoes?

GROW IT

In this age in which nearly every product is prepackaged and bears no more resemblance to its original state than a toothpick does to a forest, it is no wonder that even the origins of a dish of steamed carrots are somewhat of a mystery to the child—and perhaps to us all. Most children know that the food on the table is prepared from what comes from the market. It somehow came to be "someplace else," but exactly where and how is rarely revealed. And what happens to the leftovers? Or to the bits and pieces of food that never meet the stove or table?

The following simple and fun activities increase the child's appreciation of exactly how our "daily bread" comes to be. This appreciation should give rise to a greater desire to make the most of what nature gives us, even to the point of taking better care of our throw-aways.

More Food from Old Food

SETTING THE STAGE
Invite the children to consider the many possible ways food is grown:

Have you ever wondered where food comes from? You probably know that all or most of the food in your house comes from the store, but where did the store get it?

All food comes from something that was grown in the ground. This is even true for meat because the animals people eat also eat plants.

Perhaps you've had your own garden which you started from seeds or tiny plants. But what would you say to planting *garbage*? Of course, you can't plant *all* your throw-aways and come up with something you can eat, but if you know what you are doing, you can grow many things that are quite tasty.

WHAT YOU'LL NEED
1. Jar at least 4 or 5 inches tall
2. Water
3. 1 carrot
4. Knife

5. ½ dozen toothpicks
6. 6-inch flowerpot
7. Potting soil

HOW TO DO IT
1. Fill the jar with water.
2. Cut off the top inch of the carrot.
3. Poke several of the toothpicks into the sides of the carrot top.
4. Place the carrot top in the jar so that the toothpicks are resting on the rim of the jar. Be sure the cut part of the carrot is touching the water.
5. Place the jar in a sunny place indoors.
6. Check the jar each day to make sure the carrot is always in water. Note any changes.
7. When the roots are several inches long, plant it in the pot with the potting soil. Keep it in the sun and water it regularly.
8. While you're waiting for the harvest, read *The Carrot Seed* by Ruth Kraus.
9. When the leaves are 8 to 10 inches long, pull up the whole plant—and see what's become of last month's throw-aways!

What Else

Explain to the children that because the carrot grows completely underground, it is called a *root*. Let them try this same growing method using other roots and see what happens. Or try it with one of the biggest seeds in the world, the avocado pit. Simply wash it and stick some toohpicks around its middle. Put the rounded end in the water, and watch the changes. When the root is several inches long and you can see tiny root hairs growing out of it, plant it in a container of potting soil. When it outgrows the pot, plant it in a large spot in the backyard. (Outdoor planting works best in warm climates.)

Sprouting Seeds and Beans

SETTING THE STAGE
Invite the child to imagine what happens to the seed between the time it enters the soil and the time it emerges as a growing plant:

> If you have ever planted a garden from seeds, you know that after you put the seeds in the ground, you have to wait a long time before the plant starts to grow. (Or at least that is the way it seems.)

> If you could see inside the soil, you'd see that a lot goes on with that little seed when you're not looking.

WHAT YOU'LL NEED
1. Quart jar
2. 1 tablespoon alfalfa seeds
3. Water
4. 6-by-6-inch piece of cheesecloth
5. Rubber band

HOW TO DO IT
1. Put the seeds in the jar and fill it one-quarter full with water.
2. Stretch the cheesecloth over the top of the jar and secure it by putting the rubber band around the rim.
3. Place the jar inside a cupboard.
4. The next day, pour out the water, keeping the cheesecloth in place. Rinse the seeds with water 3 or 4 times.
5. After the final rinse, make sure all of the water has dripped out of

the jar. Place it on a windowsill or some other spot where it will receive sunlight for most of the day.

6. Follow the same rinsing procedure for the next 4 days, rinsing each morning and evening.

7. On the fifth day, rinse the sprouts and put them in a plastic bag or other container in the refrigerator to keep them fresh. They're delicious—and nutritious—in soups, sandwiches, salads, or just by themselves.

What Else

Now that the youngsters have had a glimpse of what goes on in their gardens before the seeds see the sun, they can follow this same procedure with any seeds they can think of. They can even use sprouts to decorate their homes: Have the child cut a sponge into a pretty shape, soak it with water, and put it in a saucer. Sprinkle some seeds on the sponge and watch the sponge garden grow.

All seeds and beans sprout in the same orderly way. Challenge the children to find others to sprout. Remind them that although sprouts are great to eat alone or in combination with other things, they are also baby plants, which makes this project a great way for the children to start their very own gardens.

For even more ideas, read *Growing Plants from Fruits and Vegetables* by Jane Sholinksy.

CHOOSE IT

When asked to select foods for a meal, children might name the last delicious thing they ate, or perhaps something that was just advertised on television. Obviously, the more possibilities there are available, the more intelligent will be the child's decision.

The following activities will show the child what good foods are available for meals and snacks. What makes these activities especially enlightening is that the children's natural interest in food will bring them to scientific investigation of its origins. What's more, through these activities, the children will also come to know why we eat what we eat and how to choose our favorite foods accordingly.

While gaining technical knowledge about the food we eat, the children will be actively involved in exercising not only their personal food preferences but their knowledge, which has been expanded by this newly discovered information.

Roots, Bulbs, Seeds,
and Leaves You Can Eat

SETTING THE STAGE

Invite the children to think of familiar terms in new ways and to learn to categorize the food they eat in a special way:

> When we think of roots, we usually think of what is under trees that keeps them from falling over. Bulbs are what we put in lamps or (if you have a green thumb, perhaps you know this) they are what causes certain flowers, like tulips or daffodils, to grow in the spring. Seeds are what gardeners plant and birds eat, and leaves are what make trees pretty. But did you know that you could eat these things, too?

> So the next time you're hungry, if you would just think of *these* things, you could come up with lots of good things to eat!

WHAT YOU'LL NEED
   1. Writing paper
   2. Pen or pencil
   3. Dictionary
   4. Crayons or colored pens

HOW TO DO IT
   1. For each category, have each child do the following: Write the name of the category (root, bulb, seed, leaf) on the top of a sheet of paper.
   2. Look up that word in the dictionary and read the definition to the children.
   3. Have the children write down a simplified version of the appropriate definition under each category.
   4. Let the children take turns naming foods that fit each description. Have them draw and label the foods on the appropriate pages.
   5. Staple the pages together to make a book.

What Else

The children have just discovered where much of our food comes from, and in what form. Perhaps they would now like to make a collage of magazine pictures, drawings, and even real examples of these foods, which are both good to eat and beautiful to look at.

When they are done with this portion of the activity, they are sure to be hungry, so offer them a hearty selection of tasty roots, bulbs, seeds, and leaves that they can eat!

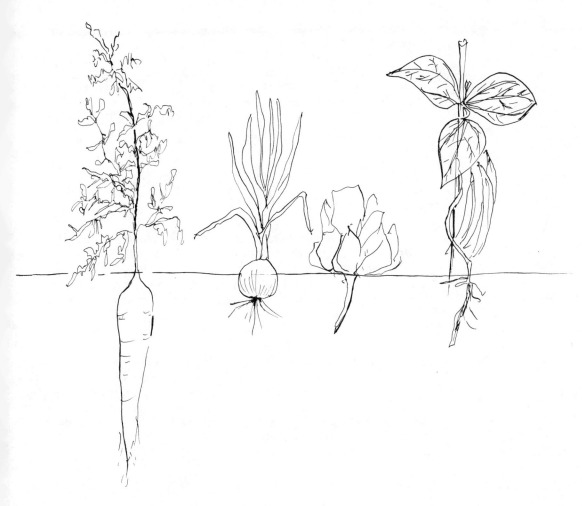

Selecting the Foods
That Make You Grow

SETTING THE STAGE

Invite the children to discover the "whys" of their daily meals:

> While eating is a great thing to do to get rid of hunger pangs, there is a much better reason for eating than to simply do away with an uncomfortable feeling. Our bodies need certain things to make them grow and go. These things are protein, carbohydrates, vitamins and minerals.

> We can't just buy little packets of these things, so we eat the foods that have these *nutrients* in them. These foods, which we need to eat every day, can be divided into four basic groups: milk products, fruits and vegetables, meats, and breads and cereals.

In order to give our bodies all the nutrients we need, we have to do more than just eat. We need to do some thinking and planning.

WHAT YOU'LL NEED

1. Large piece of posterboard
2. Marking pens in four different colors
3. Yardstick
4. Food magazines, or any magazines that feature articles on cooking
5. Scissors
6. Paste

HOW TO DO IT

1. Section off the posterboard into four equal parts.
2. Using a different colored pen for each group, label each box at the top: "Milk Products," "Fruit and Vegetables," "Meats," and "Breads and Cereals."
3. Using the same color coding system, list the types of food in each group. Make this list to the side of each quadrant so there will be enough room for pictures.
4. Cut out from the magazines pictures that represent foods from each group and place them in the appropriate quadrants.
5. In the bottom of each quadrant, note how many portions of each group are needed each day: Milk—3 to 4 servings of milk, cheese, or ice cream; Vegetables and Fruit—4 portions including citrus fruit and yellow and green vegetables; Meats—2 portions of meat, fish, poultry, eggs, or legumes (i.e., soy beans, peas, lentils); Cereals—4 servings of enriched bread, pasta, rice, or hot or cold cereal.

What Else

Engage the children in a discussion of the insights they have just gained into the "whys" of the food we all eat every day. Suggest that, from now on, whenever they want to select food for a meal or snack, they can sneak a look at the food chart first to check the possibilities. With the knowledge gained in this activity, the children can even help a busy mom or dad with the weekly menu plan and grocery shopping.

The more the boys and girls use the food chart, the easier it will be for them to remember all of the members of the food groups. One way to increase their familiarity with them is to have the children collect pictures of favorite foods which they can put together into books such as "Friends from the Milk Group" or "Favorite Cereals I have Known."

The children may also enjoy playing the "Food Guessing Game" as a means of reinforcing their new knowledge. The child who is "it" thinks up a food, and gives a clue in this form: "I'm thinking of

something to eat that grows underground and tastes good in sandwiches for lunch." The others take turns asking questions about the food until they have enough information to guess what it is, such as: "Does it have a shell?" "Must something be done to it before it goes into the sandwich?" "Which food group does it fit into?"

(Oh yes. In case you haven't guessed, the answer is "peanut.")

Finally, to get a free poster, "Nutrients and Foods for Health," send a postcard to USDA, Room 3405, Auditor's Building, 201 14th Street SW, Washington, DC 20250.

COOK IT

From the time they are old enough to walk, children are fascinated with cooking. As toddlers, girls and boys alike delight in mixing imaginary ingredients into make-believe cakes and pies anywhere from the sandbox to the bathtub. As preschoolers, the youngsters will enthusiastically help mom or dad with even the most simple cooking chore.

In the following group of activities, you can channel this natural interest into a purposeful and ordered introduction into the art and science of cooking. The recipes are designed to emphasize the special transformation that takes place when one ingredient mixes with another—or the magic that happens when a single ingredient is prepared a special way. (You'd be surprised how many young connoisseurs of "quick cuisine" are baffled when the ubiquitous "fries" are accidentally called potatoes.)

The recipes are further designed to teach rudimentary techniques. Many of them are recipes that all but the smallest child can perform on an individual basis from start to finish. In other recipes, the various steps in the procedure can be divided up as best suits the interests and capabilities of the children in your group.

Whether the child takes a full or partial role in the preparation of the food, however, the young cook will be left with a practical insight into the basics of the culinary arts. This input will work to stimulate further creativity. The child will continue to experiment with food, and because this experimentation will be based on accurate knowledge of cooking techniques, the results will probably be successful. This, in turn, will encourage not only the future gourmet in each child, but the budding scientist as well.

An unrelated, but nonetheless important, result of this group of activities is that the children will experience a renewed appreciation of food. They are sure to enjoy whatever they have had a hand in preparing. They will be less likely to become bored with old foods and more likely to try new foods. Those of us who have had to deal with a finicky eater on a regular basis will instantly realize that this last benefit may be the greatest one of all!

Making Things with Flour

SETTING THE STAGE
Invite the children to explore the magic that can happen when you mix flour with different ingredients.

Here is a secret about flour: It can turn into just about anything, depending on what you mix it with.

38

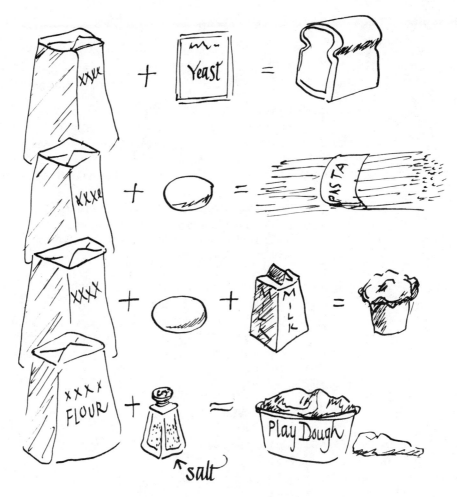

Flour contains a lot of B vitamins, the vitamins that keep us strong. Because so many things we eat every day are made from flour, we call flour a *staple*.

In the following recipes, we're going to mix flour with yeast, with eggs, and with salt. Each time, the flour will turn into something quite different—from something you can eat with baloney to something you can't eat at all!

Bread (flour plus yeast)

WHAT YOU'LL NEED

1. 1 cup warm milk
2. 1 package dry yeast
3. 1 tablespoon sugar
4. 3½ cups flour, any kind
5. 1 tablespoon salt
6. A little more flour

7. Measuring cup
8. 2 large mixing bowls
9. Large spoon
10. Clean towel
11. Bread pan

HOW TO DO IT

1. Sprinkle the yeast on ¼ cup warm milk.
2. When the yeast has dissolved, mix the sugar into it. Let it stand about 5 minutes, or until the mixture starts to bubble.
3. Mix the flour and salt in the mixing bowl. Add the yeast mixture and the remainder of the milk.
4. Stir the mixture until it holds together.
5. Begin kneading. Sprinkle some flour on your hands to keep the dough from sticking. Knead for 7 to 10 minutes. Older children will enjoy taking turns.
6. Put the kneaded dough in a clean mixing bowl. Cover it loosely with a towel. Let it rise until it has doubled in size, about 2 hours.
7. Preheat oven to 425 degrees.
8. Punch the dough down and place it in an oiled loaf pan. Let it rise once again until it reaches the top of the pan.
9. Bake at 425 degrees for 30 minutes.

Noodles (flour plus eggs)

WHAT YOU'LL NEED

1. 2 cups flour
2. ½ teaspoon salt
3. 3 eggs
4. Extra flour
5. Fork
6. Mixing bowl
7. Rolling pin
8. Knife

HOW TO DO IT

1. Mix the flour and salt together in a large bowl.
2. Make a well in the top of the flour and break the eggs into it.
3. Beat the eggs vigorously with a fork, incorporating the flour into them.
4. When the dough is soft and sticky, begin kneading as for bread dough.
5. Divide the kneaded dough into 4 or more parts, depending on the number of children.
6. Roll each part into a flat and very thin sheet (about ⅛-inch-thick).

7. Let each child carefully roll up each sheet lengthwise and cut it into pieces about ¼ inch wide. Carefully *unroll* the cut pieces.
8. Let the noodles dry about ½ hour before cooking them.
9. Cook in boiling salted water until tender, about 4 minutes.

Playdough (flour plus salt)

WHAT YOU'LL NEED
1. 4 cups flour
2. 1 cup salt
3. 4 teaspoons vegetable oil
4. Food coloring
5. Water
6. Large plastic container with lid

HOW TO DO IT
1. Mix flour, salt, and oil in a container.
2. Add food coloring.
3. Slowly add water. Continue mixing with your hands until the playdough is the favored consistency.
4. Cover the container to store the playdough.

Making Things with Milk

SETTING THE STAGE

Invite each child to discover the fact that milk is the basis of many different foods:

Did you know that you could *eat* milk?

Milk is the main ingredient in foods that you eat all the time, like butter, cheese, or yogurt.

You can also make delicious drinks with milk that are as filling and good for you as a whole meal.

Curds and Whey

WHAT YOU'LL NEED
1. 1 quart milk
2. Juice of 1 lemon
3. Large saucepan
4. Spoon
5. Small sieves (one for each child)

HOW TO DO IT
1. Pour the milk into the saucepan and bring it to a boil. Once it has boiled, remove it from the heat.

CURDS

Pour milk into pan

Bring to boil

Stir in juice of 1 lemon

Stir until milk separates into _thick_
   white lumps and watery liquid

Pour Curds and Whey through sieve

Squeeze out the liquid

Eat Curds like
   cottage cheese

2. Stir in the juice of 1 lemon.
3. Keep stirring until the milk separates into thin, watery liquid (the
   whey) and thick white lumps (the curds).
4. Pour the curds and whey through the sieves. Squeeze out all the
   liquid.
5. Eat the curds like regular cottage cheese. And beware of spiders!

Yogurt

WHAT YOU'LL NEED
1. 1 quart milk
2. 2 tablespoons powdered milk
3. 1 tablespoon homemade or commercial nonpasteurized plain yogurt
4. Saucepan
5. Spoon
6. Ovenproof ceramic casserole with lid
7. Small bowl

HOW TO DO IT
1. Mix the whole and powdered milk together in a saucepan. Slowly bring it to a boil. Stir while cooking.
2. Pour the hot milk into the casserole. Cool to 110 degrees.
3. Spoon the yogurt into a small bowl. Mix a little of the cooled milk into it. Pour this mixture back into the casserole.
4. Stir the yogurt-to-be until it is smooth.
5. Cover the casserole. Keep it at 110 degrees for 3 to 5 hours, or until thickened. (You can place it in a low oven, on top of a heating pad, or on an electric warming tray to maintain this temperature.)
6. Refrigerate when thickened. Serve plain or topped with fresh fruit.

Breakfast in a Glass

WHAT YOU'LL NEED (For Each Serving):
1. 1 tablespoon frozen orange juice concentrate
2. 1 egg
3. 1 cup milk
4. Choice of: ½ banana, ½ cup fresh strawberries, ½ cup ripe cantaloupe, or any other soft, ripe fruit
5. Blender
6. Tall glass

HOW TO DO IT
1. Pour the works into the blender.
2. Blend until frothy.

Making Things from Meat, Fish, and Poultry

SETTING THE STAGE

Invite the children to investigate new methods of cooking and *non*cooking:

> When we think of supper, we usually think of having some form of meat, fish, or poultry. These foods contain lots of protein, the nutrient that helps kids grow, and iron, the nutrient that keeps kids strong. That's why we try to eat them several times a week.
>
> These foods can be cooked—and even *not* cooked—in many different ways. Here are three new ways you can try yourself.

Shish Kebab

WHAT YOU'LL NEED (For Each Serving)
1. ¼ cup oil
2. Juice of ½ lemon
3. Salt, pepper
4. 5 1-inch cubes boneless lamb or beef
5. 4 cherry tomatoes
6. 4 mushrooms
7. 1 small bell pepper
8. Bowl
9. Knife
10. Skewer
11. Barbecue or broiler
12. Basting brush

HOW TO DO IT
1. Mix the oil, lemon juice, salt, and pepper in a bowl. Add the meat.
2. Wash the tomatoes and the mushrooms and put them in the bowl.
3. Quarter the bell pepper and put the pieces into the bowl also.
4. Let the ingredients marinate about 1 hour.
5. Alternately thread the meat and the vegetables on the skewer.
6. Barbecue or broil about 9 to 12 minutes, turning and basting with the marinade as the shish kebab cooks. (Restrict this step to adult or older children.)

Seviche

WHAT YOU'LL NEED (For Each Serving)
1. 1 small whitefish fillet
2. 2 fresh, ripe limes
3. Small shallow bowl
4. Knife

HOW TO DO IT
1. Rinse and dry the fish and cut it into chunks. Place them in the dish.
2. Squeeze the lime juice over the fish chunks until the fish is *covered* with lime juice.
3. Refrigerate overnight. The citric acid in the lime juice will "cook" the fish as surely as an oven would!
4. Eat it as is, or drain it and eat it on toast or crackers.

Baked Drumsticks

WHAT YOU'LL NEED (For Each Serving)
1. 1 plump drumstick
2. 1 teaspoon butter
3. ¼ orange
4. Small baking pan or pie plate

HOW TO DO IT
1. Wash and dry the drumstick.
2. Melt the butter in the baking pan.
3. Rub the drumstick all over with the orange. Press hard.
4. Put the drumstick in the baking pan. Squeeze the rest of the orange juice over it.
5. Bake at 375 degrees for 35 minutes.

Making Things with Fruits and Vegetables

Invite each child to conceive of simple fruits and vegetables as building blocks from which many fancier foods can be made:

Fresh fruits and vegetables give us all the special vitamins we need each day. They are so good that we usually eat them just as they are, either raw or plainly cooked.

Sometimes, however, it is fun to try new things with fruits and vegetables. Here are a few surprises.

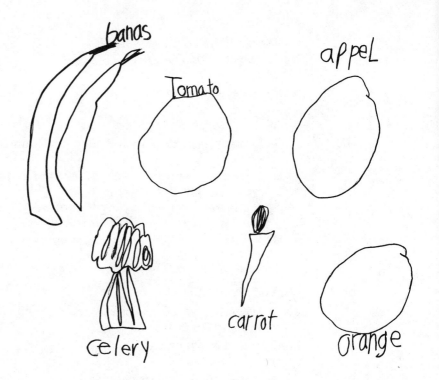

bamas

Tomato

appeL

celery

carrot

orange

French Fries

WHAT YOU'LL NEED (For Each Serving)
1. ½ potato
2. Cold water
3. Salt
4. Vegetable oil
5. Potato peeler
6. Knife
7. Large bowl
8. Paper towels
9. Small skillet
10. Slotted spoon

HOW TO DO IT
1. Peel the potato. Slice it into thin strips.
2. Put the strips into a bowlful of cold, salted water as you slice them.
3. Heat 1 inch of vegetable oil in the skillet.
4. Dry the potato slices with paper towels.
5. When the oil is hot, carefully slide the potatoes into it.

46

6. Let the potatoes cook about 8 minutes, until they look crispy. Stir occasionally with a slotted spoon.
7. Remove when cooked and drain on paper towels.

Leftovers Soup

WHAT YOU'LL NEED (For Each Serving)
1. 1 cup milk
2. 1 tablespoon flour
3. 1 tablespoon butter
4. ½ to 1 cup leftover (or precooked) vegetables
5. Blender
6. Saucepan
7. Spoon

HOW TO DO IT
1. Put all the ingredients into the blender. Process until smooth.
2. Pour the mixture into the saucepan.
3. Cook, stirring, on medium heat until the mixture is thickened and bubbly.

Mix-up Salad

WHAT YOU'LL NEED (For Each Serving)
1. 1 apple
2. 1 stalk celery
3. 1 carrot
4. ¼ cup chopped nuts
5. 1 tablespoon lemon juice
6. 1 tablespoon mayonnaise
7. Knife
8. Bowl
9. Spoon

HOW TO DO IT
1. Wash and cut the apple into chunks.
2. Wash and slice the celery.
3. Scrape and slice the carrot.
4. Toss all the ingredients in the bowl. Mix until all the nuts, apples, and vegetables are coated with the lemon juice and mayonnaise.

Sherbet

WHAT YOU'LL NEED
1. 1½ to 1¾ cups sugar
2. 1 cup water

3. 2 egg whites
4. 3 cups pureed fruit (any mashable fruit, but preferably berries)
5. Saucepan
6. Spoon
7. Mixer
8. Ice trays

HOW TO DO IT

1. Combine the sugar and water in the saucepan. Bring it to a boil and cook—stirring all the time—until the sugar dissolves. Remove from heat.
2. Beat the egg whites until stiff.
3. When the sugar syrup has cooled, add it to the egg whites. Beat well.
4. Add the fruit. Mix it up well.
5. Pour the soon-to-be-sherbet into icetrays, and freeze until hard.
6. Remove the sherbet from the freezer a few minutes before serving to soften slightly.

What Else

Now that the children have discovered the wonders of cooking, they are sure to want to pursue the magic techniques further.

One way to continue stimulating a growing interest in cooking is to teach the youngsters to make their own recipe books. This project will not only increase their awareness of different flavors and processes but will also encourage experimentation.

To make a recipe book, each child will need a notebook, pen or pencils, crayons or marking pens, and pictures of food cut out of magazines. For each recipe, write the name of the food on the top of the page and draw (or cut and paste) a picture of it. Have the child note when and where the food was first eaten, what kind of food it is ("dessert," "salad"), how long it takes to prepare, how easy or difficult it is to prepare, and how much cleanup is involved. (It's never too early to teach boys and girls that cleaning up is an integral part of the cooking process.) Then list the ingredients in order of use, the tools and utensils required, and, finally, the instructions. Older children might wish to convert the lists of ingredients, utensils, and instructions into simple illustrations. (In fact, they may even want to translate the recipes in this chapter into visual form as an enjoyable and valuable exercise in conceptualization and as an equally valuable service to the nonreaders in your group.)

Be sure to impress upon the children the ease with which recipes can be obtained. Nothing would please a parent more than to hear a formerly finicky eater finish a meal someday with a "Thanks, that was great. Can I have the recipe?"

The adage "It's not what you do, but how you do it" was probably never more true than in the case of food. Try serving a boiled turnip all alone in the middle of a plate and note the reaction. Then, on the next day (if your family is still speaking to you), try tossing a couple of these boiled roots into a batch of mashed potatoes. Garnish with parsley and a cherry tomato, and you may well have a hit on your hands—at least you've improved your chances.

Or in the case of something more appealing but still a bit mundane, like vegetable soup, float some grated cheese, croutons, or sprouts on top to add much-needed and appreciated variation on an all-too-common theme.

Even the tastiest of food is more apt to be eaten with pleasure (indeed, eaten at all) when prepared and served with all of our senses in mind and not just that of taste. Just see what happens, for example, when you serve Chinese Crackling Rice Soup. If children's educations are maximized by a multisensory approach, why not enhance their daily meal in the same way?

A child's sense of self-sufficiency will grow when meals are served with utensils he or she can use properly and in an aesthetically pleasing setting. A child's sense of beauty will grow when meals are served artistically, and the eyes of even the most avid peanut butter and jelly fan will sparkle in a new way when that sandwich takes on the form of a teddy bear or a heart.

By introducing the child to the creative side of serving food, we do more than supply a daily dose of nutrition. We are able to introduce a new and often sweeter side to food, and we are able to generate new interest in creating beauty and variety in our daily experiences.

Finger Foods

SETTING THE STAGE

Invite the children to discover the meaning—and the fun—of "Finger Foods"

What are your favorite foods? What do you use to eat them? What if you sat down to a meal and all you had in front of you was the food—no spoons, no forks, no plates? Then what would you do?

As you can imagine, this would be a disaster if you had a hot fudge sundae in front of you. But there would be no problem if you had a sandwich, because you could eat that with just your hands. Well, just your fingers, to be exact.

There are a lot of foods you can eat that way. We have a special name for them, and you can surely guess what that name is. You guessed it—*finger foods!*

Finger foods are really handy because you can fix them and eat them all by yourself.

Finger Sandwiches

WHAT YOU'LL NEED (For Each Serving)
1. 2 slices bread
2. Peanut butter or sliced cheese
3. Cookie cutter
4. Knife

HOW TO DO IT
1. Cut the bread with the cookie cutter. If you're using cheese, cut that, too.
2. Spread the peanut butter or place the cheese between the two slices of bread.

Fruit or Vegetable Kabobs

WHAT YOU'LL NEED (For Each Serving)
1. Several pieces of fruit or vegetables.
2. Skewers, which may be purchased or fashioned from straws or toothpicks. (If you use toothpicks, you can make "sculptures" rather than the standard linear layout.)
3. Knife.

HOW TO DO IT
1. Slice the fruit or vegetables into bite-sized pieces. Be sure to leave the peel on whenever possible. That's where many of the vitamins cluster.
2. Skewer the fruit or vegetables in an attractive pattern.

Individual Pizza

WHAT YOU'LL NEED (For Each Serving)
1. 1 English muffin
2. 1 tablespoon butter
3. 3 tablespoons tomato paste
4. 4 olives
5. 4 tablespoons grated mozzarella cheese
6. Salt, pepper, and herbs as desired
7. Knife

HOW TO DO IT
1. Toast and butter the muffin halves.
2. Spread the tomato paste evenly on the buttered sides of the muffin.

3. Slice the olives and place them on the muffin halves.
4. Sprinkle the cheese on top. Add seasonings, if desired.
5. Bake at 400 degrees until the cheese is melted (about 10 to 15 minutes).

What Else

Now that the children have discovered what "finger foods" are all about, turn them loose in the kitchen. (Make sure they understand that they will have to clean up the mess afterward!) Challenge them to surprise *you* with a snack, then retreat to the bedroom, garden, or lounge with a good book for a few minutes. If the children need a little help, you might lay out a selection of ingredients on the table before you abdicate. Remind them that the beauty and design they can create with finger food is ultimately as limitless as the beauty and design in nature which gave us this food. Then wait for the results. You probably will be most pleasantly surprised, if not with the exact nature of the snack, at least with the creativity and love with which it was prepared.

Making It Look Nice

SETTING THE STAGE

Invite the child to think of the best-looking food imaginable:

What is your favorite food? What do you like best about it?

What if you went to a restaurant that had food you had never tasted before and, to make your choice, all you had to go on was the way the food looked? What would your choice look like?

As you've been thinking about these questions, you have probably discovered something. It's a lot more fun to eat something that looks pretty. And could it be that when it looks nice, food actually tastes better, too?

WHAT YOU'LL NEED

1. Small scraps (3 by 5 inches or smaller) of construction paper in as many colors and hues as you can find
2. Paste
3. A midday meal or dinner
4. A tray of garnishes (for example, small pieces of vegetables and fruit)

HOW TO DO IT

1. Spread out the scraps of paper on the table.
2. Let the children shuffle through the paper. Have them put different color combinations together until they find especially appealing ones. Have them paste these last scraps together in an overlapping pattern so all the colors are visible.

3. When each child has several color combinations selected, serve the meal.

4. Let each child garnish his or her meal with the appropriately colored fruits or vegetables in a way that duplicates one of the favored color combinations as closely as possible.

5. When the children have finished eating, ask them to plan some hypothetical meals of foods and garnishes that have pleasing color combinations. For example, zucchini might be lots more fun to serve and eat when it is sprinkled with kernels of bright yellow corn.

What Else

Now that the children are familiar with the possibilities of color in cooking and garnishing, they can be even more creative by making up their own designs. For example, raisins can turn a scoop of cottage cheese into a face. Fruit or vegetable garnishes can be made fancy by peeling a strip or two along the outside or by cutting scallops and zigzags along the edges.

EAT IT

Different Teeth for Different Treats

An ounce of prevention is truly worth the proverbial pound of cure when it comes to teeth. With just a few simple additions to our daily routines, we can be virtually guaranteed a lifetime with our very own sets of healthy teeth and gums.

In the following activity, the child will gain a new understanding of the "why" of teeth. This knowledge will be interesting and fun to discover. As a result, teeth will become as familiar to the child as the food they help to digest. And as we all know, it is always easier to care for something we know something about.

Once the main activity is complete, you might want to help the children brush up on dental care techniques, like brushing—teeth, gums, and tongue—and flossing. At this age, children are especially fascinated with the idea of dental floss, and will learn to use it in no time.

Armed with this newly discovered knowledge about teeth and how to care for them, the child will hopefully be on the road to a lifetime of good oral hygiene. The effects of this will be long-lasting and will reach beyond the immediate goal of dental care: If the child does indeed maintain good dental habits day by day, he or she will also be increasing personal responsibility in caring for basic health needs. What greater reward for the effort than that of the youngster's own well-being?

SETTING THE STAGE

Invite the child to participate in a "firsthand" exploration of teeth:

Are your hands clean?

Put your fingers in your mouth and run them along your teeth. What do you feel? Do all the teeth feel the same? Why do you suppose your teeth feel the way they do?

Is all the food we eat the same? What do you think is the reason for all this variety in one little mouth? Let's try an experiment to discover the answer.

WHAT YOU'LL NEED
1. A piece of beef or chicken (small enough to pick up with your hands, but larger than bite-sized)
2. A large, crunchy lettuce leaf

HOW TO DO IT
1. Have the children take a bite of meat, chewing it with their front teeth only.
2. Have them do the same thing using only their back teeth.
3. Repeat the first two steps with the lettuce.
4. Ask the children which teeth did the best job on the meat? With the lettuce?

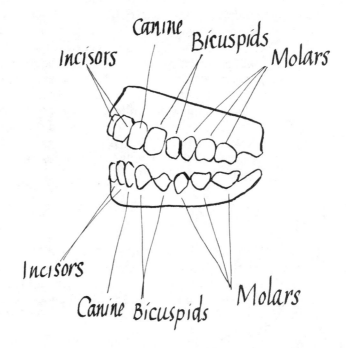

5. Tell the children this: You have just discovered why nature gives different animals different kinds of teeth. Sharp, pointy teeth, like our front teeth, are good for ripping and tearing, which is what meat eaters *(carnivores)* do when they dine. Those animals who are strictly vegetarians *(herbivores)* have flat teeth for grinding. As you've probably already realized, humans eat *both* kinds of food (that makes us *omnivores).* So we need both kinds of teeth.

What Else

The children may want to make booklets to record what they have learned about their teeth. They might also want to list the animals that fit into the carnivore/herbivore categories, just by looking at pictures of these animals that show their teeth. To get the children started, ask them whether Bugs Bunny is a carnivore or an herbivore.

While you are on the subject of teeth, do remind the children about brushing and flossing. Though most children brush every day, not all of them know the proper way to do it. And very few children have ever been shown how to floss. Following your demonstration, you might want to try this experiment that will show the children another way to care for their teeth while eating a meal, even one that includes arch-enemy number one—candy!

Pass out a carrot, a piece of sticky candy, and a glass of water to each child. Have them take a bite of carrot, a bite of candy, and a sip of water in rotation until all the food and water is gone. Ask them to take special note of how their mouths and teeth felt after eating or drinking each item. Did their teeth feel slick? Did their mouths feel gooey? The moral of the story (or of the experiment) is this: Whatever leaves one's mouth feeling slick and shiny is good for the teeth. So the next time a meal contains something sugary or chewy, follow it up with something hard, like a carrot, or something slick, like an ice-water chaser.

Finally, invite the children to start their own dental health libraries by writing to the Bureau of Health Education, American Dental Association, 211 E. Chicago Avenue, Chicago, IL 60611. Ask for copies of "Casper's Dental Health Activity Book" and "The ABCs of Good Oral Health."

STORE IT

Preservative has become one of the dirtiest words in the consumerist lexicon. Yet, in this context, it is a misnomer. For preservative—or preservative measures—are always needed to keep food at its freshest. What may *not* be needed are the chemicals that have come to be used as preservatives in many of our processed foods.

The following group of activities focuses on preservatives in the most natural sense of the word. The children will first learn to determine the difference between fresh and spoiled food; in the process they will get practice in the scientific method. The boys and girls will then participate in two of the oldest methods of preserving food: canning and drying.

On the most practical level, the "Store It" activities will give the youngsters practical information that they can put to good use around the house. Hardened cheddar and soggy Grahams, for example, should be spoils of the past soon after the children participate in "Experiments with Freshness." Once they learn to recognize the difference between good and spoiled food, they will be less likely to suffer the effects of food that has gone bad.

Experiments with Freshness

SETTING THE STAGE

Invite the child to observe the special care that must be taken to insure that foods stay fresh:

> Are the foods in your lunch box packed a certain way? Did you ever wonder why?
>
> All foods need special protection to stay fresh. When foods are fresh, they taste better and look better. But most important, they are better for you, too.
>
> Some foods, like the milk in your thermos, must be kept cold. Others, like your sandwich, must simply be wrapped. Still other foods, like fresh fruits, are equipped with hard skins so that they can stay fresh on their own.
>
> It is important to store foods properly so that they stay fresh as long as possible. Here are some experiments that will show you how.

Experiment 1: Soft Things

WHAT YOU'LL NEED
1. 1 slice of fresh bread
2. Knife
3. Plastic wrap

HOW TO DO IT
1. Cut the bread in half.
2. Wrap one half in plastic.
3. Expose the two halves to air overnight.
4. Ask the children for their conclusions from this experiment.

Experiment 2: Crisp Things

WHAT YOU'LL NEED
1. 1 Graham cracker
2. Plastic wrap

HOW TO DO IT
1. Break the cracker in half.
2. Wrap one half in plastic.
3. Expose both halves to the air overnight.
4. Ask the children to draw their conclusions from this experiment.

Experiment 3: Crunchy Things

WHAT YOU'LL NEED
1. 1 stalk celery
2. Knife
3. Plastic bag

HOW TO DO IT
1. Cut the celery in half.
2. Put one half in the plastic bag.
3. Leave both halves on an open refrigerator shelf overnight.
4. Ask the children to draw their conclusions from this experiment.

Pickles and Preserves

SETTING THE STAGE

Invite the children to conceive of ways to keep *large* amounts of food fresh:

Suppose you had four big baskets of peaches. How long would it take your family to eat them all up? Do you think they would stay fresh that long?

Sometimes, no matter how careful we are, we have more food than we can possibly eat before it goes bad. So, rather than wasting the food, we must do something to *preserve* it, or keep it fresh until we *can* eat it.

One way to preserve fruit is to cook it and add sugar to it. This is how you make jelly or jam.

A way to preserve vegetables is to add salt and vinegar to them. Do you know what is made by this process? Pickles!

Easy Dill Pickles

WHAT YOU'LL NEED
1. 4 to 6 small, fresh cucumbers
2. 2 sprigs fresh dill
3. 1 teaspoon alum
4. 1 teaspoon pickling spice
5. 1 cup vinegar
6. 2 cups water
7. 1½ tablespoons salt
8. Large sterilized jar
9. Small pot

HOW TO DO IT
1. Soak and scrub the cucumbers.
2. Put the dill, alum, and pickling spice into the jar.
3. Pack the cucumbers into the jar.
4. Bring the vinegar, water, and salt to a boil.
5. Pour the boiling brine over the cucumbers in the jar.
6. Cover tightly and refrigerate. The pickles will be ready to eat in a few days and will keep for several weeks in the refrigerator.

Peach Jam

WHAT YOU'LL NEED
1. 2 pounds peaches
2. 1 tablespoon lemon juice
3. ½ cup water
4. 1½ cups sugar
5. Knife
6. Large pot
7. One or two large sterilized jars

HOW TO DO IT
1. Peel and slice the peaches.
2. Put them into the pot along with the lemon juice and water.
3. Cook over medium-low heat until the peaches are soft.

4. Add sugar. Cook, stirring, until mixture thickens, about 20 minutes.

5. Pour the jam into the jars, cover and refrigerate. The jam will keep for about one month.

Drying Fruit

SETTING THE STAGE

Invite the children to investigate another way to preserve food:

Fresh air draws moisture out of food. It causes foods to dry up or wilt. That's why it is their enemy.

Sometimes, though, it can be their friend. Drawing moisture out of food also draws out tiny moisture-loving plants called *bacteria*, which can cause food to spoil. So drying can be a way to preserve food, too.

Some foods that are especially yummy when they are preserved by drying are fruits. Dried apples, bananas, or apricots are quite good, as are dried grapes, which you probably eat all the time! Did you know that they were raisins?

Delicious as dried fruits are, however, you must remember that drying also causes the fruit to lose some of its vitamins. So, though dried fruits are good to eat for treats, fresh fruits are still better for you.

WHAT YOU'LL NEED

1. Fresh fruit, preferably fruit that is not quite ripe
2. Knife
3. Large, clean tray
4. Cheesecloth, nylon net, or a clean screen

HOW TO DO IT

1. If the fruit has a hard skin, peel it. Carefully remove the seeds. Core apples whole.
2. Slice the fruit into ½-inch-slices. (If you are drying apples, the slices will be shaped like doughnuts. If you are drying apricots, simply break apart the halves.)
3. Lay the slices on the tray. They should not be touching.
4. Put the tray outside in the hot sun. Cover it with cheesecloth, net, or screening to keep unwelcome visitors off.
5. As soon as the sun goes down, bring the tray in to a warm dry part of the house.
6. Repeat the process until the fruit is leathery and chewy (about 3 days).
7. Store the dried fruit in airtight containers.

What Else

Now that the children have experimented with freshness and preservative measures on a practical level, they might be ready for a little more input on a cerebral level. Here are some avenues of discussion:

As the children discovered in their experiments, air causes food to lose its proper texture either by drawing out its moisture or by making it soggy. How can air do these two seemingly opposite things at once? The answer is *homeostasis,* a rather formidable word which means the tendency of all things—in this case, moisture molecules—to seek their own equilibrium. Since the fresh bread, for example, contains more moisture than the air, the air draws moisture from the bread. Conversely, the air contains many more particles of water than does a cracker, so the cracker draws moisture out of the air and thus becomes soggy.

Wrapping and refrigerating are two ways to protect foods from the ravages of the air. There are others, however. Soaking cut or peeled vegetables in salt water, for example, will keep them fresh. And coating cut or peeled fruit with lemon juice will keep the edges from turning brown.

Bacteria, which are present in all foods, are the villains that cause food to spoil. If you want to keep food fresh for any length of time, you must prevent bacteria from taking over. Bacteria are fair-weather friends; though they multiply rapidly at room temperature, they grow very slowly in cold temperatures. And in freezing temperatures, they don't grow at all. Another way to stop their growth is to completely eliminate the two things they need for survival, air and moisture.

If you want to kill bacteria outright, you must heat the food to high temperatures. This is the basis for the canning method of preserving foods.

Cooking food to make jam or pouring boiling brine over vegetables effectively kills whatever bacteria are present at the time, and the pickles or jam will stay fresh *in the refrigerator* for a long time. However, to prevent any new bacteria from entering the food, you must "seal" the filled and sterilized jars by processing them in a hot water bath.

Of course, pickles and jams are not the only way food is canned. Ask the children to name some others. Canning foods, or "putting them up," was the major way of preserving food in the days before refrigeration, and it is still the main way we can be assured of having some fruits and vegetables—and some seafoods—all year long.

You might wrap up this discussion by asking the children how they can tell if a particular food is fresh enough to eat. How is it packaged, for example, or where has it been kept? When in doubt, teach the youngsters to use the eye, ear, nose, and tongue test: Is the food the right color? Does it "crunch" if it should? Does it smell nice? And does it taste good?

PICK IT YOURSELF

For most children, experience with food begins at the supermarket and ends at the dinner table. Now, these boys and girls are bright enough to realize that green beans don't grow in supermarket bins, yet rare is the child in this day and age who has had the opportunity to tangibly relate to green beans in their natural habitat.

An outing to a pick-it-yourself farm or ranch will be an exciting learning experience for children of all ages. At the most immediate level, the youngsters will delight in taking an active role in bringing their food to the table. By carefully choosing the ripest, choicest fruits or vegetables, the children will naturally increase their appreciation of the food being picked, whether it is a strawberry or a radish. The outing will also expose the children to many aspects of horticulture. Practical lessons in irrigation, planting techniques, or even pest control are just waiting to be taught. Finally, by getting in touch with the origins of a special food in this little trip "back to nature," the children's spirit of adventure and resourcefulness will necessarily grow.

Once the trip is over, you can use the bounty to put the techniques learned in the "Store It" section to practical use. What's more, you can

use this outing as a gateway to introductory discussions of communal sharing, trading, and, eventually, commerce.

SETTING THE STAGE

Invite the child to bypass the market in discovering where fresh foods come from:

> Do you have any fresh fruit in your lunch today? Did you have any fresh vegetables for dinner last night?
>
> Where did they come from?
>
> Of course, they probably came out of the refrigerator in your kitchen, but where did they come from before then? The supermarket? How did they get *there?*
>
> No matter where we buy them, all fruits and vegetables come from farms. These farms can be large or small, close to where we live or far away.
>
> Farmers spend all year growing these yummy foods. They pick them when they are ripe and ship them to the supermarkets, where *we* can pick them out of a bin and take them home.
>
> Would you like to have an adventure? Let's visit a farm where we can pick our *own* fruits and vegetables right off the plants where they grow!

WHAT TO DO BEFORE YOU GO

1. No matter how urbanized your area is, there are sure to be a few small ranches or farms nearby. Especially during the summer, these farmers are happy to have people come and pick their own produce. Frequently, these places will advertise in local papers or post signs along the highway. You can also telephone your local Chamber of Commerce or Agricultural Commissioner for information.

2. When you find out what and where you will be picking, get picture books that will help you explain the particular fruit or vegetable's growing cycle and growth pattern to the children.

3. Explain the concept of "in season" to the children. Give examples of fruits and vegetables that are in season now and ones that are not.

4. Have everyone dress in old, dark-colored clothes the day of the harvest. If it is summertime, make sure the redheads and blondes wear either sunhats or sunscreens.

5. Bring paper bags, boxes, or baskets if necessary.

WHAT TO DO WHILE YOU'RE THERE

1. Walk around the farm or ranch if you can. Point out the rows in which the fruits or vegetables were planted. Find the irrigation system. Help the children imagine exactly how much fresh food is growing right before their eyes.

2. Demonstrate to the children the proper way to pick. Show them

how they can tell the good, ripe fruit or vegetables from the ones that aren't quite ready.

3. Give each child a container . . . and start picking!

WHAT TO DO AFTERWARD

1. Talk about how you will store the fruit or vegetables and how long they will keep.
2. Discuss ways to cook the fruit or vegetables.
3. Decide what to do with the pickings. The children will surely want to share their produce with their families. However, if there is an abundance, you might want to make a pie, jam, or pickles.
4. Invite the children to accompany you on a make-believe voyage to the days before the advent of the supermarket. Where would food come from? Would everyone have to be a farmer? Would there be sharing and trading among neighbors? How would everyone get enough to eat?
5. Let each child make a booklet or chart to trace the growing cycle of a favorite fruit or vegetable from seed to maturity.
6. Investigate the growth patterns of unusual edible plants like artichokes, Brussels sprouts, or even peanuts. Try to imagine how and why the first one ever got eaten!

VISITS TO THE FOOD PROCESSORS

The nature of the child is to wonder, and this is good, for this is precisely how the child learns.

Because we adults have been exposed to this world of ours for so long, it is sometimes hard for us to realize how mysterious some of the most ordinary things can be for little children.

Take, for example, a can of creamed corn. The child may know that the corn originally grew on an ear on a stalk. But what mystifies the little one is how the corn ever got into the can. Or, for that matter, why?

A visit to a cannery, a commercial bakery, or a dairy can solve untold mysteries for the questioning child and, in so doing, bring the child that much closer to an understanding of the many things that go on in his or her world. This field trip is an excellent way, in fact, to wrap up the investigation of food that took place in the preceding pages. The children will be able to observe in large scale many of the techniques practiced in their own kitchens. They will delight in witnessing the "from nothing to something" process that takes place right before their eyes, and will undoubtedly be awed by the assembly line.

In short, the visit to the food processor will provide the children with the final piece of the puzzle of where their food comes from. By seeing how milk is processed or how hot dog buns are baked, the children will come to an understanding of how many of the foods that they eat eventually come to their table.

SETTING THE STAGE

Invite the child to discover how and why packaged foods come to be:

> We have learned how to prepare many nutritious and delicious foods. We have seen how many different fruits and vegetables grow. But sometimes there are foods that we just can't make or just can't grow ourselves.
>
> These are the kinds of foods that come in packages—like sacks of flour or loaves of French bread, for example, or half-gallons of low-fat milk, or cans of creamed corn. Where do you suppose these foods come from?
>
> Throughout our country, there are many factories where whole foods, like grains or cow's milk or corn on the cob, are processed, or prepared, for us. Large bakeries package thousands of loaves of every kind of bread each day. Dairies start with fresh cow's milk, then process it into milk, yogurt, and butter that will stay fresh for many days. And canneries "can" any kind of vegetable or fruit—and even meat or fish—that you can imagine so that we are able to enjoy these foods no matter what the season.
>
> Have you ever wondered where all the foods in the supermarket with the brightly colored labels come from? Let's go see.

WHAT TO DO BEFORE YOU GO

1. Call your local Chamber of Commerce to find the names of food processors in or near your town. Call the public relations department of each of these companies, asking if it would be possible to arrange a tour for some well-behaved young boys and girls.
2. Ask the children to name all the foods they can think of that come in packages or are "processed" foods. Explain that processed food is food that has been changed from its original form in some way.
3. When you have chosen a food processor to visit, ask each child to find a book, a recipe, a label, or a special picture that relates in some way to this particular food.
4. Discuss the materials that the children have found. Then trace the food from its raw state to its most processed form.
5. Have the youngsters bring paper and pencils.

WHAT TO DO WHILE YOU'RE THERE

1. Look and listen! There probably will be a guide assigned to conduct you on your tour.
2. Point out the ingredients and processing techniques that might be familiar to the children as points of reference.
3. If there is an assembly line, make sure the children observe in what an orderly way the production proceeds from one step to the next. (Most children are fascinated with the precision of

assembly lines and, at this point, may even want to work on one when they grow up!)

4. Encourage the children to take notes or draw pictures of whatever is most interesting to them.

5. If there is an opportunity to do any tasting, by all means do! Be sure to sample foods that look or smell unusual.

WHAT TO DO AFTERWARD

1. Make a chart of the processing you observed, from the raw ingredients to the final labeling.

2. Discuss the technique that was used and, if possible, compare it to a food activity, such as baking bread or making yogurt, that you have shared.

3. If there was an assembly line to watch, talk about the way it worked. If you have a group of children with you, set up an assembly line to perform a simple cooking task, such as making shish kebab.

4. Talk about what would happen if there were no food processors. For example, if there were no canneries, when could you eat tomato sauce or sliced peaches? If there were no dairies, what would you need in your backyard to put milk on your table each evening? And if you wanted sandwiches for lunch, what would you have to do every morning?

5. If any child has an especially favorite processed food—anything from a particular brand of yogurt to a special candy bar—write to the company. (You'll find the address in small print somewhere on the label.) In all probability, you'll receive a packet full of information on how the product is made and where. There may even be a factory to visit near you!

BOOKS FOR CONTINUING DISCOVERY

Books for Adults

BURNS, MARILYN. *Good for Me.* Boston: Little, Brown, 1978.

LANSKY, VICKI. *Feed Me, I'm Yours.* New York: Bantam, 1979.

LANSKY, VICKI. *The Taming of the C.A.N.D.Y. Monster.* Wayzata, Minnesota: Meadowbrook Press, 1980.

SHAY, ARTHUR. *What It's Like to Be a Dentist.* Chicago: Reilly and Lee Books, 1972.

Books for Children

ELLISON, VIRGINIA. *The Pooh Cookbook.* New York: Dutton, 1969.

HOBAN, RUSSELL. *Bread and Jam for Frances.* New York: Harper & Row, Pub., 1964.

KRAUS, RUTH. *Carrot Seed.* New York: School Book Service, 1971.

LORD, JOHN VERNON. *The Giant Jam Sandwich.* Boston: Houghton Mifflin, 1972.

SENDAK, MAURICE. *Chicken Soup with Rice.* New York: Scholastic Book Service, 1962.

SHOLINKSY, JANE. *Growing Plants from Fruits and Vegetables.* New York: Scholastic Book Service, 1974.

CHAPTER THREE

MOTOR DEVELOPMENT / THE BODY

AN APPLE FROM THE TEACHER

The adult who leads children in motor development faces a special and ultimately rewarding challenge. Here is a unique experience that creates the perfect environment in which children may learn new skills, increase social awareness, improve organizational abilities, and delve into the mysteries of human body. They can even ready themselves to read! All this may be done indoors or out, rain or shine, and in the best possible way—active play.

Activities in this chapter mark an exciting departure from traditional movement exploration. With each activity, the child will gain increased body awareness and knowledge of how that miraculous body works. Each activity is used to demonstrate a principle of human physiology in the same way in each section. This allows the child to focus on the function of that particular part of the body without being unduly distracted by the process of learning a new game.

Each "lesson" speaks to children in the way they most easily understand—play. This special knowledge easily translates into playtime activity. In doing so, the girls and boys learn new ways to have fun. Once they have played hopscotch four different ways, for example, thinking of a fifth alternative (or maybe even a whole new game!) will be a snap.

While the children are busy exercising the bodies they have come to know so well, growth is taking place on a subtle, inner level as well. The children are helping their minds to think and their bodies to perform on a more sophisticated level than before. Simple games such as "Teacher-May-I?" require the child to mentally organize and then physically act out a series of motions. This innocent play has a direct and very profound effect on the child's ability to perform more abstract cognitive functions, such as recognizing a sequence of letters to make a word and then putting together several of those words to express a complete thought.

Understanding this intimate relationship between motor and cognitive development will quickly dispel the "bookworm" and "jock" stereotypes. It is no mere coincidence that Rhodes scholarships are awarded to those who exemplify excellence in body as well as mind. Growth toward maximum potential necessarily involves growth in *all* areas of an individual's needs and interests. Motor development activity affords children a special opportunity to simultaneously meet the needs of mind and body.

THE CARE AND FEEDING OF LARGE MUSCLES

Children will "play outside" by the hour, engaging in unlimited forms of active recreation. They play because it's fun.

As concerned and loving adults, we love to have our children go out to play. Admittedly, at times our motives are less than noble. For example, we welcome sending the children outside to provide time when we can regain a measure of our own equilibrium through solitude. However, we also appreciate active play as a means of relieving the children of excess energy that, if allowed to build up, could easily spell disaster by midafternoon.

And yet the youngsters' active play does more for their inner development than the superficial observer could ever imagine. Active play lays the groundwork for socialization. It is this very interaction that gives girls and boys practice in the skills that will help them relate to their peers throughout their lives. In addition, active games can be obvious, empirical measures of a child's self-worth. The typical five-year-old boy can jump rope ten times after one week of practice, twenty-five times the second week. He quite deservedly feels good about his success, and thus, himself. Likewise, the sandlot slugger who, after days of practice, finally smashes her first one over the fence has a feeling of achievement. These measurable improvements bring an undeniable sense of well-being to the children. They are exhilarated mentally and emotionally, as well as physically.

The activities in this section are designed to help children identify those parts of their body that make active play possible—the large muscles. They will learn how these muscles work and will play several games that emphasize their development and that help the children realize the important role these "big movers" play in everyday activity.

SETTING THE STAGE

Invite the children to learn about muscle structure:

> Did you play outside yesterday? What are your favorite outside games?
>
> What do you suppose it is that lets you play these outdoor games? Your mom or dad or your teacher, of course, let you go outside to play. But what else?
>
> If you said your muscles, you're right! All people, even little children, have hundreds of muscles in their bodies. Their job is to make you move.
>
> You have two kinds of muscles. Large muscles and small muscles. The large muscles are the big movers that do big jobs, like helping you run, or lift, or throw. Here is how they work. Each muscle is made of many fibers. You can think of it as a bundle of strands of spaghetti. When the muscle is relaxed or not working, the strands are long and soft, like cooked spaghetti. When the muscle goes to work, the fibers tighten so they are hard and short, like uncooked spaghetti.
>
> When you run or play, these fibers take turns working so that none of them get too tired too soon. But even so, when you have been playing for a long time, they still get tired. So you stop playing and take a rest.
>
> To increase your muscles' strength, or the amount of time they can work without pooping out on you, you must take care of them with plenty of good food, good rest, and, most importantly, exercise.
>
> Like dodgeball, or jumprope, or hopscotch, or relay races . . .

Finding the Big Movers

WHAT YOU'LL NEED

1. Xerox copies (if possible) of Figure 3-1a and b for each child
2. Crayons

HOW TO DO IT

1. Point out the following large muscle groups on the charts, and give examples of the jobs they do:
   - *Abdominal muscles* hold tummies in.
   - *Back muscles* help you lift and throw.
   - *Chest muscles* help you lift and throw.

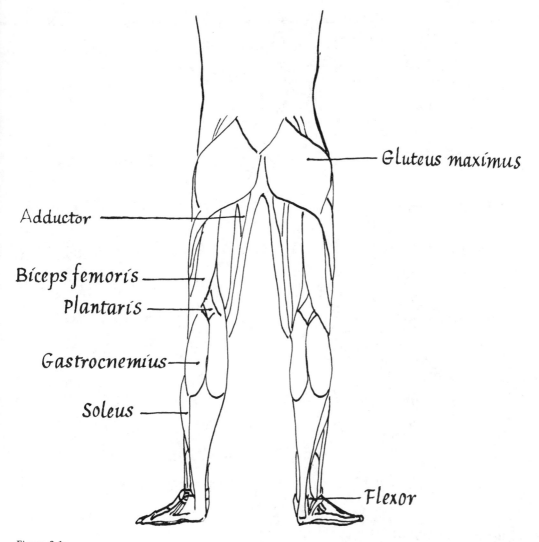

Gluteus maximus

Adductor

Biceps femoris

Plantaris

Gastrocnemius

Soleus

Flexor

Figure 3-1a.

- *Upper arm muscles* help you turn a jumprope.
- *Upper leg muscles* help you walk, run, and jump.
- *Lower leg muscles* help you walk, run, and jump.
2. Let the children color in each muscle group as you point it out.
3. Help the boys and girls isolate their own large muscle groups as they do these simple movements:
   - *Abdominal muscles:* Push under belly button.
   - *Back muscles:* Cross arms tightly in front of you.

69

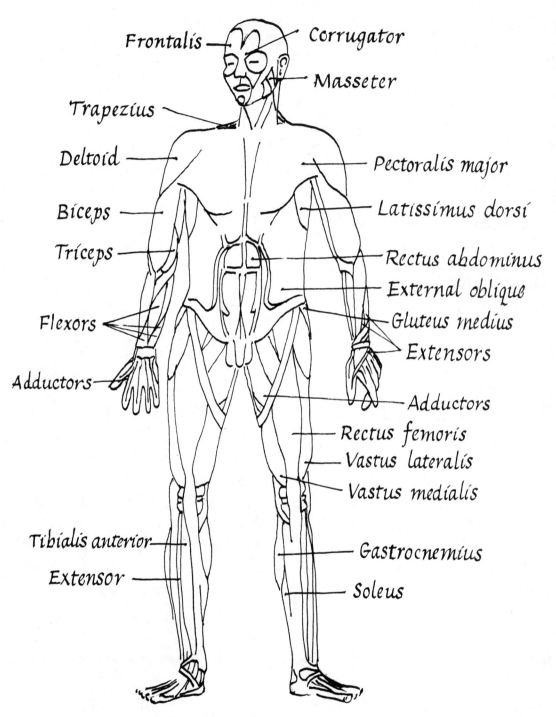

Frontalis

Corrugator

Masseter

Trapezius

Deltoid

Pectoralis major

Biceps

Latissimus dorsi

Triceps

Rectus abdominus

External oblique

Gluteus medius

Flexors

Extensors

Adductors

Adductors

Rectus femoris

Vastus lateralis

Vastus medialis

Tibialis anterior

Gastrocnemius

Extensor

Soleus

Figure 3-1b.

- *Chest muscles:* Bring elbows together behind you.
- *Upper arm muscles:* Bend elbows and place hands on top of head.
- *Upper leg muscles:* Stand straight, then bend knee up.
- *Lower leg muscles:* Stand on tiptoes.

Feeding the Big Movers

WHAT YOU'LL NEED (For Each Child)
1. ¼ cup shelled peanuts
2. 1 slice whole wheat bread
3. 1 tablespoon butter
4. Milk
5. Plastic bag
6. Rolling pin
7. Knife

HOW TO DO IT
1. Explain to the children that muscles need protein to grow, and that a snack of peanuts, whole wheat bread, and milk is good "protein food."
2. Put the shelled peanuts into the plastic bag.
3. Crush the peanuts with the rolling pin until they are very finely ground.
4. Spread the butter on the bread. Top with the crushed peanuts. Fold the bread in half.
5. Accompany the snack with a glass of milk.
6. Ask the children which large muscles they used in making their snacks.

Games to Keep Large Muscles Busy

Hopscotch

WHAT YOU'LL NEED
1. An expanse of flat cement
2. Chalk

HOW TO DO IT
1. Draw your favorite hopscotch pattern on the ground.
2. Allow the boys and girls to play as they ordinarily do, but ask them which large muscles propel them through their game.

Calisthenics

WHAT YOU'LL NEED
1. Some open floor space

HOW TO DO IT

1. Demonstrate your favorite large muscle exercises to the children. (This will benefit you as much as the kids!) Here are some suggestions: sit-ups, leg lifts, push-ups (modify the standard push-up by lying face down with knees bent upward), and deep knee bends. Large-muscle-strengthening exercises like these should be done with abrupt movements to clearly define the muscle-tightening process.
2. Have the children exercise along with you. Ask them which muscle groups are working in each exercise.
3. Set up a regular exercise schedule for you and the children.

Relays

WHAT YOU'LL NEED

1. Open space
2. Balls

HOW TO DO IT

1. Divide the children into teams.
2. Mark off the "course."
3. Try these three relays:
   • Have the children leapfrog their way to and from the baseline.
   • Have the children crawl on all fours to and from the baseline.
   • Have the children bounce a ball to and from the baseline.

Teacher-May-I?

WHAT YOU'LL NEED

1. Some open space

HOW TO DO IT

1. The "teacher" calls the children in random order and commands each to advance from "home" toward "school" by taking 5 baby steps, 2 giant steps, 8 twirly steps, and so on. In order to advance, however, the child must name the large muscle group or groups that make the movement possible. The first child to reach "school" becomes the next "teacher."

Jumprope

WHAT YOU'LL NEED

1. A long, sturdy rope

HOW TO DO IT

1. Make sure the children take turns *turning* as well as jumping! If you run short of kids, you or a cooperative tree can fill in at one end.

2. The number of jumprope games is endless. For example, any song or rhyme with alternating stress/nonstress beats can be converted to a jumprope chant. After the first round, either repeat the chant for the next jumper or simply count the jumps until the first jumper misses.

3. For more inspiration, read *Jump the Rope Jingles* by Emma V. Worstell.

Dodgeball

WHAT YOU'LL NEED

1. A wide open space
2. A ball, preferably not too hard (a Nerf Ball, if possible)

HOW TO DO IT

1. Divide the children into teams.
2. One team makes a wide circle. The other team goes inside the circle.
3. The outside team tries to hit an "insider" with the ball; the insiders try to dodge the ball. When a player is hit, that child is out. When all the insiders are out, the teams switch positions. (Caution the children not to throw the ball too hard.)
4. A variation for smaller groups is balltag. The child who is "it" tags another child simply by throwing the ball at, and hitting, that child. This player is then "it."

What Else

What condition are *your* muscles in? If you have good muscle tone, you might like to "flex" your muscles for the children, and let them feel the difference between relaxed and tightened muscles.

Older children, or those especially interested in physiology, may want to know more about how muscles work. Here's what you can tell them: Muscles are designed to make bones move. They are fastened to the bones at either end by *tendons*. Muscles work across *joints;* quite simply, they make the bones move by making the joints move.

Muscles also work in teams. For every muscular pull, there is an opposing counterpressure to keep the original motion under control. For example, when you bend your arm up toward your face, one muscle gives you the strength to raise your forearm while the other members of this muscle team pull back to prevent you from punching yourself in the nose!

Big and small children alike may want to make a chart of all their muscular movements throughout a typical day. Have them record the various activities they do, such as walking to school, playing baseball, or carrying groceries, and then note the muscles that were called on to perform.

As a wrap-up activity, have the children trace Figure 3-1b along the heavy outer lines, then very carefully outline and color in the large muscle groups with one color. Have the boys and girls keep their finished work in a safe place.

You'll see why later.

(To ensure children's safety as they develop the big movers, make sure they are familiar with basic first aid skills. For free booklets on first aid, send a postcard to: Consumer Services, Johnson and Johnson, 501 George Street, New Brunswick, NJ 08903. Ask for "First Aid for Little People" and "First Aid Guide.")

THE CARE AND FEEDING
OF SMALL MUSCLES

To an enormous extent, our tools of communication reside in our small muscles. The muscles in our face and throat allow us to speak; those in our hands allow us to write. Correspondingly, we use these muscles to learn—to question, to turn the pages of a book, to examine things on a tactile level. And we dearly need the small muscles located in our feet to get us from here to there as we conduct our lifelong exploration of the world around us.

It is no wonder, then, that children's small muscle development coincides with the first stages of intellectual refinement. The growth of fine motor skills allows young children increasingly accurate expression of their inner selves. As their fingers grow in dexterity, they express themselves by scribbling, by building with blocks, by drawing, and, finally, by writing. They learn to speak with clarity and to walk or run with agility. Happily, this is a self-perpetuating growth process.

As the youngsters objectively measure their increased accomplishment, they are encouraged to push on; they continually work to refine these small muscle skills, and their intellectual processes sharpen accordingly.

In effect, small motor development enhances a child's opportunity for intellectual growth. It allows a frictionless flow of creativity that is both natural and essential to the growing human being. And, as any child will surely tell you (especially after completing the following activities), the more developed the small muscles are, the more fun a kid can have!

SETTING THE STAGE

Invite the children to consider the importance of the small muscles in refining movement:

> Can you wiggle your toes? How about your nose? Do you know what is responsible for these movements?
>
> Your small muscles are. Just as you have large muscles that do large jobs, you have small muscles that do small jobs. It really isn't fair to call these jobs "small," though, because they can be the most important ones of all.
>
> For example, your large muscles may give you the strength to carry a bag of groceries into the house, but it is the small muscles in your hands that help you pick up the bag in the first place and then hang onto it until you can put it down on the kitchen table.
>
> In other words, large muscles give you the *strength* to do lots of things, but, in most cases, it is those small muscles that put that strength to work for you.
>
> Many of your small muscles are located in your *extremities.* That's a fancy way of saying that the closer you get to your hands, feet, or head, the more likely you are to find a small muscle or two. There are small muscles in your head to help you talk, eat, and make faces. There are small muscles in your feet to help you balance. And of course, there are small muscles in your hands to help you do hundreds of useful things.
>
> So now you know how important the smallest guys on the team really are. Want to learn more about them?

Finding the Smallest Guys on the Team

WHAT YOU'LL NEED

1. Xerox copies of Figure 3-1b for each child
2. Crayons

HOW TO DO IT

1. Point out the following small muscle groups on the chart and give examples of the jobs they do:
   - *Facial muscles* help you chew and whistle.

• *Hand muscles* help you write, grasp, and snap.
• *Foot muscles* help you walk and run.

2. Let the children color in these muscle groups as you point them out.
3. Help the children isolate their own small muscle groups with these simple movements:
   • *Facial muscles:* Wink, chew, flare nostrils, thrust jaw out, repeat "la, la, la" several times rapidly, try to whistle.
   • *Hand muscles:* Grasp a finger of the opposite hand, move each finger in turn independently of the other four on each hand.
   • *Foot muscles* (best done with bare feet): Wiggle toes; stand on tiptoes; take two very slow steps, rolling the foot from heel to toe.
4. Ask the children to notice which of the movements in this section can be made independently of large muscles—that is, with legs, arms, neck, or back relaxed and still.

Feeding the Smallest Guys on the Team

WHAT YOU'LL NEED (For Each Child)
1. 2 slices whole wheat bread
2. Butter or mayonnaise
3. 1 slice sandwich meat
4. 1 slice cheese
5. Knife

HOW TO DO IT
1. Refresh the children's memories. Tell them that muscles (even small ones) need protein food.
2. Trim the crusts from the bread.
3. Spread the bread with butter or mayonnaise.
4. Lay the sandwich meat and cheese on one slice and top with the other.
5. Make sure the sandwich is perfectly aligned.
6. Cut the sandwich into three strips to make—what else—"finger sandwiches."
7. Ask the children how many small muscles they might use to make finger sandwiches. Where are these small muscles located?

Games to Keep Small Muscles Busy

Hopscotch

WHAT YOU'LL NEED
1. An expanse of flat cement
2. Chalk

HOW TO DO IT

1. Draw the same hopscotch pattern you drew for the previous hopscotch game.
2. Let the children play as before, but this time ask them to name the *small* muscles that help them play their game.

Calisthenics

WHAT YOU'LL NEED

1. Some open space
2. Mirrors
3. A bright lamp
4. An open wall

HOW TO DO IT

1. Sit or stand so that each child can look into a mirror. Then make faces! Let each child take turns choosing a face to be made. Don't neglect wiggly ears, floppy tongues, or twitchy noses!
2. Set up a bright light about 5 feet away from an open wall. Make shadows on the wall by moving fingers in front of the lamp. Can anyone make a bird? A swan?
3. Sit in a circle on the floor with legs outstretched and bare feet facing inside the circle. Have the children take turns doing things with their toes that the others must copy, such as crossing one over the other, picking things up, or pinching the toes of one foot with the toes of the other. Try not to move from the ankles up.

Relays

WHAT YOU'LL NEED

1. Open space
2. Balls
3. 2 shopping bags, each containing a complete outfit (pants, shirt, shoes, hat) of old, larger-than-kid-size clothes, with the outfits matched in terms of buttons, zippers, and so on.
4. Chalk or pens and paper

HOW TO DO IT

1. Divide the children into teams.
2. Mark off the course.
3. Try these relays:
   - Have the children run to and from the baseline while tossing a ball into the air and catching it.
   - Have the children run to the baseline, dress and undress in the old clothes, and run back.

• Have the children run to the baseline, write their names with chalk on the sidewalk or with a pen on paper and run back.

Teacher-May-I?

WHAT YOU'LL NEED

1. Some open space

HOW TO DO IT

1. Make this twist on the traditional "Teacher-May-I?" You be the first teacher. In order to advance, each child in turn tells the teacher what movement he or she would like to make. The hitch is that the child must not only name a movement that utilizes a small muscle group, but must correctly locate it. For example, the child might say, "Teacher, may I take five hopping steps which use the small muscles located in the front of my foot?"
2. The first child to reach the school becomes the next teacher.

Toe the Line

WHAT YOU'LL NEED

1. Open space
2. Chalk or masking tape

HOW TO DO IT

1. Mark off a long, wiggly course with one continuous line.
2. Let the children play follow-the-leader on the course. No matter what the movement, at least one foot (or hand, if they get really fancy) must be balanced on the line at all times.

What Else

There are any number of games that help develop small muscle control in children. Unfortunately, however, they require more in the way of equipment than simply good weather and willing participants. Among them are jacks, marbles, tiddlywinks, pick-up-sticks, and any kind of card game.

You might also like to try some activities that reinforce the importance of small muscles in a negative way. For example, have the children attempt to walk like dolls, without moving their feet or ankles. Or fill a tray with small objects and have the boys and girls see how many they can pick up *without* using any finger muscles.

Finally, take out those diagrams you made at the end of the section on large muscle activity. Have the children lay them over Figure 3-1b so that the body contours are aligned, and then trace the small muscles onto this same sheet. The children should use a different color for these muscles.

THE CARE AND FEEDING OF BONES
AND JOINTS AND THINGS

If you've ever peered inside a ballet class on a college campus, you may have noticed a number of men and women exercising at the bar who looked more like athletes than dancers. In all likelihood, appearances were *not* deceiving: Those who looked like athletes were probably members of the football, basketball, tennis, or even golf teams.

Most likely, these students were sent to class by their coaches—not necessarily to learn ballet, but rather to increase their flexibility and balance. Ballet classes entail hours of exercises designed to stretch muscles to the limit so that dancers can move their bodies with exquisite precision and balance. These attributes are obvious necessities on the dance floor, yet they're equally important on the fifty-yard line, too.

Though flexibility is a function of muscle conditioning, it is also a direct measure of how well we are able to move our bones and joints. The more flexible we are, the better we are able to perform—anywhere from the tennis court to the front stairs—and the less likely we are to do ourselves injury.

The following group of activities includes a wide selection of exercises and games that will increase children's natural flexibility while adding to their knowledge of the inner structure of the human body. As the children participate in the activities, they will become aware of the ways in which they can and cannot move. What's more, they will get a tactile lesson on the order of the human frame. The children will discover where their "moving parts" are located, how this hardware is arranged, and what goes on inside it.

The way the body works will begin to make sense to the child. Perhaps an interest in medicine will be sparked, or an aptitude for gymnastics discovered. What is sure is that you and the children in your care will discover even more new ways to enjoy outdoor play.

SETTING THE STAGE
Invite the girls and boys to discover their movable parts:

> Squeeze your arm. Do you feel something hard inside? Something that keeps your arm from flip-flopping all over like a bowl of jelly? Can you guess what this hard something is?

> If you said "bone," you're right! You have many bones all over your body. They are hard and stiff, like hollow pipes. They are the parts of you that move.

> Now bend your arm at the elbow. Think about this: If the bones are the parts of you that move, and if bones are hard and stiff, how in the world did you bend your arm?

The answer, of course, is that your elbow is a *joint.* A joint is like a hinge that connects one bone to another. Joints allow you to do important things like bending, twisting, pointing, pivoting—even clenching your fist or grasping your pencil.

Of course, all the bones and joints in the world won't get you from bed to breakfast unless your muscles are working, too. Muscles are fastened to bones by *tendons,* which allow the muscles to take your bones where you want them to go.

You may be thinking that your "hardware" must be pretty busy keeping you moving all day. You're right. But as a bonus, these bones and joints and things perform one more important service for us. Inside bones, there is a substance called *bone marrow,* which manufactures the red blood cells we all need to live. What's more, bones—as hard and stiff as they are—are alive and growing.

But you probably knew that already. How else could you outgrow your jeans so fast!

Finding the Hardware

WHAT YOU'LL NEED
1. Xerox copies of Figure 3-2 for each child
2. Crayons
3. Rag doll

HOW TO DO IT
1. Point out the major bones and joints on the chart. (Gauge the extent of this step—the number of bones you identify and the names you use—to the attention spans and interest levels of the children.)
2. Let the children color in each bone or joint as you mention it.
3. Help the children discover their own bones and joints by feeling for them. Using the chart as a guide, demonstrate on your own body, then invite the children to do the same. Be sure to include the skull and the ribcage. On slender children, you may even be able to count the ribs.
4. Help the children locate their joints this way: Face the children, holding the rag doll in front of you. Move the doll every which way. If the children can copy the doll's movement, ask them which joint allowed them to move that way.

Feeding the Hardware

WHAT YOU'LL NEED (For Each Child)
1. 1 cup milk
2. 1 scoop vanilla ice cream

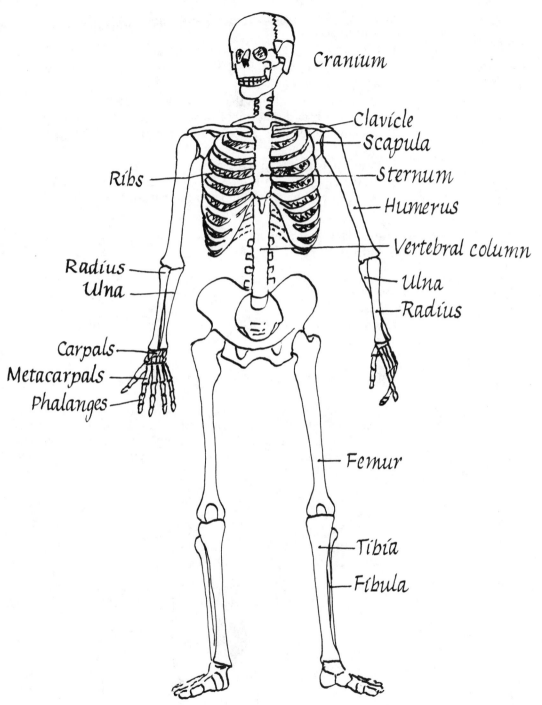

Cranium

Clavicle

Scapula

Sternum

Humerus

Vertebral column

Ulna

Radius

Ribs

Radius

Ulna

Carpals

Metacarpals

Phalanges

Femur

Tibia

Fibula

Figure 3-2.

3. ½ cup fresh strawberries, fresh banana, fresh peach, or other fruit in season
4. Blender
5. Glass

HOW TO DO IT
1. Explain to the children that *calcium* is the substance that makes bones hard, and that milk is a great source of calcium.
2. Toss the ingredients into a blender. Blend 5 to 10 seconds at high speed.
3. Pour the contents into a glass.
4. As the children are drinking their shakes, ask them if they can figure out other snacks to keep the hardware healthy.

Games to Keep Bones and Joints and Things Busy

Hopscotch

WHAT YOU'LL NEED
1. An expanse of flat cement
2. Chalk

HOW TO DO IT
1. Draw the same hopscotch pattern as in the previous hopscotch games.
2. Invite the children to play by the same rules as in the original game with this exception: They must 'hop' by holding the raised leg straight out to the side or in front rather than bending the knee. (This variation emphasizes the fact that the knee is a very handy joint to have.)

Calisthenics

1. Some open floor space

HOW TO DO IT
1. Children are already the most flexible of creatures. These exercises and others will help them maintain their natural flexibility and increase their coordination. Demonstrate these muscle-stretching exercises (or favorites of your own) to the children:
   - Toe touching.
   - Back rocking. (Lie on your back with legs straight. Bring your knees forward, raise your head, and clasp your hands around your legs. Rock forward and back on your spine a few times, then stretch out and repeat.)
   - Waist swiveling. (Stand straight, hands on hips. Swivel at the waist as far left and right as possible without moving your legs, then alternate raising each knee as your twist.)
2. Have the children exercise with you. Discuss the joints that are (or are not) moving in the various exercises and the muscles that feel as if they are stretching.
3. Combine these exercises with the large muscle exercises in your daily routine. Remember that stretching or flexibility exercises should be done slowly to s-t-r-e-t-c-h each muscle as fully as possible.

Relays

WHAT YOU'LL NEED
1. Open space
2. Low table
3. 2 wide-mouth jars
4. 2 large thread spools
5. 2 long, thin boards, ropes, or some masking tape

HOW TO DO IT
1. Divide the children into teams.
2. Mark off the course.
3. Try these three relays:
   - Have the children run to the baseline; chant "My knees, my shoulders, my nose, my toes," touching each point as it is named; then run back.
   - Have the children run to the baseline (where the low table is set up), pick up a thread spool, deposit it in the jar *without* moving any arm joints below the shoulder, and then run back.
   - Have the children tiptoe on the "tightrope" (designated by a board, rope, or line of masking tape) to and from the baseline without losing their balance.

Teacher-May-I?

WHAT YOU'LL NEED
1. Some open space

HOW TO DO IT
1. Play the game with this variation: Instead of telling the child what move to make, the teacher suggests only that the child take "five steps with both knees straight" or "three steps with arms raised and elbows bent."

Stoop Tag

WHAT YOU'LL NEED
1. Open outdoor space

HOW TO DO IT
1. The child who is "it" must chase the other children and tag one of them. The child who was tagged then becomes "it." The catch this time is that the children are safe from being tagged when they are in a stooping or squatting position.

Tumbling

WHAT YOU'LL NEED
1. Open indoor space with a carpeted floor

HOW TO DO IT
1. Start with somersaults: Have the children bend over, knees slightly bent, touching their head and hands to the floor. To give the novices a start, give them a tiny push forward from behind.
2. Proceed to tripods. Have the children bend over, hands flat on floor, elbows bent. Have them then raise their lower body, supporting their knees on their elbows. (This will surely take some help from you at first.)
3. A handstand is the next progression from the tripod. When the child feels secure in the tripod position, gently raise the youngster's legs up straight. Stay close! Children who can manage this position can raise themselves by straightening their arms and eventually will be able to "walk" on their hands.
4. Other tumbling exercises to try include backward somersaults, cartwheels, and the splits.
5. Show the children how much they can do with well-trained bones and joints by sharing *The Very Young Gymnast* by Jill Krementz with them.

What Else

As another activity to demonstrate the variety of positions our joints make possible, try the following game with the children. Pass out 3-by-5-inch cards and have the children draw a simple stick-figure person on each card. The figure's bones and joints can be positioned any way the child wishes, so long as that particular pose is possible to do. Collect the cards and make sure the drawings are clear, then play this game with them. Hold up a card and have all the children imitate the position. Any child who fails to do so is out. The last child left becomes the next leader.

To reinforce the knowledge the children have gained in this activity, as well as to introduce the youngsters to something new to do with bones and joints and things, send a postcard to: Capezio Ballet Makers, Department RB 79, 1860 Broadway, New York, NY 10023. Ask for "Why Can't I Go on My Toes?" and "How Can I Achieve a Dancer's Body?"

Finally, take out the diagrams from the previous two groups of activities once again. This time, place them over Figure 3-2 and invite the children to trace the major bones and joints with black ink or crayon.

THE CARE AND FEEDING
OF THE HEART AND LUNGS

With this group of activities, the child is introduced to the essential aspects of physiology—the inner workings of the heart and lungs. The girls and boys will learn, in a straightforward and simplified manner, how these vital organs operate, how to measure their performance, and where to find the conduits that help them get their jobs done.

The aura of reverence that surrounds the heart and lungs has never been lost on children. Every time a youngster sees the pediatrician, or even the school nurse, the child is poked and prodded in quest of the elusive "vital signs." The following group of activities offers children some insight into what this process is all about. The ice-cold stethoscope and the blood-pressure cuff will seem less like adversaries and more like important tools when youngsters have a greater appreciation of what's going on. (This is not to say that pediatricians will be able to lower the shoulder-high doorknobs in the examining rooms, but at least it's a step in the right direction!)

These activities will bring further discovery of how the things the children do affect these organs and the way their bodies feel in general. The result will be, hopefully, a long-lasting respect for the hardest-working members of the body team, and a lifelong dedication to preserving their well-being. The children will be introduced to aerobic exercise and will learn a few new games in the bargain. As their knowledge of the human body takes shape, the children will have the opportunity to become active participants in the maintenance of their own good health.

SETTING THE STAGE

Invite the youngsters to discover how the cardiopulminary machinery works

> Who can guess the two hardest workers in each of our bodies? These are parts that *never* take a break. They work even when we sleep.
>
> Want to know the answer? It's our heart and our lungs.
>
> The *heart* is a muscle that pumps blood to every bit of our bodies for our whole lives. The *lungs* are two spongelike sacs that fill up with air when we breathe. Without blood and air—and a special kind of air, at that—we couldn't live.
>
> The blood's job is to deliver nourishment to every cell in our bodies. One of the most important things it delivers is *oxygen.* Oxygen is the most important part of the air we breathe. Every part of our body needs it, from our head to our toes.
>
> But before the blood gets on its way to nourish toes and fingers and brain cells, the heart pumps the blood next door to the lungs. Here in the lungs, the oxygen we've just breathed in is separated from the air we will soon breathe out. The blood picks up oxygen from the lungs, then takes it all over the body. Once all the deliveries have been made, the blood returns to the heart and the process begins all over again.
>
> Blood flows through highways called *blood vessels. Arteries* are the vessels that take blood away from the heart, and *veins* are the vessels that bring it back. Most of them are hidden way below the skin where they'll be safe. *Capillaries* are very tiny blood vessels that carry the blood from the arteries to the individual cells.
>
> The airways, of course, are our nose and mouth and our windpipe (also called the *trachea),* which connects the air passages in our face directly to our lungs.
>
> When we exercise, our bodies cry out for more and more oxygen. So our heart and lungs must work faster than they usually do. That is why we breathe faster and our heartbeat increases when we exercise. This is good for our heart and lungs because it makes them stronger. The stronger they are, the easier it is for them to do their job.
>
> And that's important, because the easier it is for the heart and lungs to do their job, the longer we can play and run and jump, and the better we will feel, even when we're not playing.

Finding the Highways and Airways

WHAT YOU'LL NEED

1. Xerox copies of Figure 3-3 for each child
2. Crayons

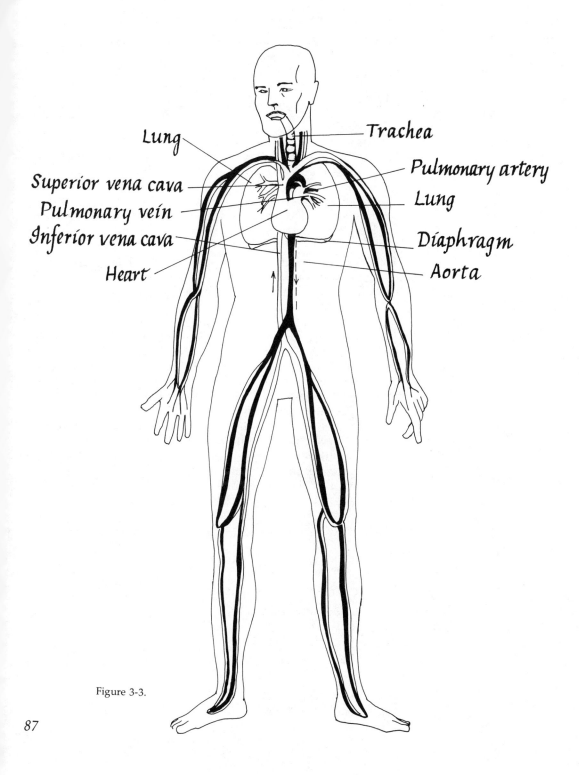

Lung

Trachea

Pulmonary artery

Superior vena cava

Lung

Pulmonary vein

Inferior vena cava

Diaphragm

Heart

Aorta

Figure 3-3.

3. Mirror
4. Watch or clock with a second hand
5. Balloons

HOW TO DO IT
1. Point out the following on the chart: heart, blood vessels, lungs, and windpipe.
2. Let the children color in each of these things on the chart.
3. Help the children find their own blood vessels. Blue veins can be seen on the underside of the forearm. Most arteries are hidden deeper under the skin, but there is a large artery in the temple that usually stands out immediately following exercise. Have the children check for this one after they've been playing hard. Capillaries are most visible in the eyelid or under the tongue. Have the children find their own by looking in the mirror.
4. The heartbeat is the sound of the heart's valves opening and closing as they pump the blood through the circulatory system. Have the children take turns listening to one another's heartbeat by holding an ear up against the middle of each other's chest.
5. The *pulse* is the feel of the blood as it pumps through the arteries. The underside of the wrist (under the thumb) is the easiest place to feel it. When the children have found their own pulse (they mustn't feel with their thumbs as thumbs have a pulse of their own!), have them count the beats for 10 seconds. Multiply these numbers by 6 and you will have their pulse rates. (Children's normal resting pulse ranges from 65 to 110 beats per minute.) Have the children take their pulse while at rest and after 5 minutes of running or jumping and note the difference.
6. Have the children put their hands on their chests. Tell them to take a deep breath and hold it, then exhale completely. Ask them if they could feel their lungs.
7. Have the children take a deep breath, then immediately blow into a balloon. This is obviously not an accurate measure, but it will give the boys and girls an idea of their individual lung capacities.

Feeding the Highways and Airways

WHAT YOU'LL NEED (For Each Child)
1. ¼ cup raisins
2. ¼ cup pumpkin seeds
3. ¼ cup sunflower seeds
4. 4 dried apricots, cut into quarters
5. 1 cup apple juice
6. Plastic bag
7. Glass

HOW TO DO IT

1. Explain that instead of feeding the highways, you will feed the blood that travels inside them. And what blood needs is lots of *iron,* which is contained in many dried fruits and seeds.
2. Mix the first four ingredients together in the plastic bag.
3. Serve with a glass of apple juice.
4. Explain that the airways need good, clean air to breathe. Ask the children where they think the best places to find clean air to breathe might be.

Games to Keep the Heart and Lungs Busy

Hopscotch

WHAT YOU'LL NEED

1. An expanse of cement
2. Chalk
3. Watch or clock with a second hand
4. Paper
5. Pencil

HOW TO DO IT

1. Draw that same old hopscotch pattern one more time.
2. Let the children play any variation of the hopscotch game. To give them an idea of how hard their hearts work during the game, however, have the children measure their pulse rates before and after each turn.
3. To calculate how play affects the lungs, have the youngsters count their breaths before and after each turn.
4. Record the "before" and "after" pulse and breath rates on a chart.
5. Ask the children if they notice any pattern in the information recorded on the chart.

Calisthenics

WHAT YOU'LL NEED

1. Open floor space
2. Record player or radio
3. Music with a steady beat

HOW TO DO IT

1. Tell the children that any type of exercise that increases their pulse and breathing rates for a long time is good for the heart and lungs. Exercises you might try are jumping jacks, running in place, and "bicycle riding." (Do the pedalling motion while lying

A Jumping jack

on your back with your feet in the air.) Demonstrate these exercises first, then have the children join you. (Guard against overexertion. Start slowly, then increase the exercise period each day.)

2. Once you and the children get used to these exercises, do them to music. Vary the arm and leg movements to avoid monotony, and try to do each exercise for at least a 5-minute stretch. (Remember, this type of cardiovascular exercise is perhaps even more important for adults than it is for kids!)

3. Incorporate these and other calisthenics you and the children are familiar with into a dance routine.

Relays

WHAT YOU'LL NEED
1. Open space
2. Balloons
3. Straws
4. Playing cards

HOW TO DO IT
1. Divide the children into teams and mark off the course.
2. Try these relays:
   - Have the children run to the baseline, blow up a balloon, let it go, then run back.
   - Have the children skip to the baseline and hop back.
   - Have the children run (or walk) to and from the baseline suspending a playing card on the end of a straw by sucking air through the other end of the straw. If the course is especially long, the children can "refuel" at the baseline by removing the straw long enough to get a deep breath.

Teacher-May-I?

WHAT YOU'LL NEED
1. A *lot* of open space

HOW TO DO IT
1. Play this old standby somewhere where there is a lot of room between school and home. Have the teacher command the children to do some sort of step—hopping, jumping, skipping—then say "go!" All the children must race to school, doing the appropriate step. The first one there becomes the next teacher.

Red Light, Green Light

WHAT YOU'LL NEED
1. Open space

HOW TO DO IT
1. Name one child "it."
2. Mark off a "home" and a "base."
3. The child who is "it" stands at the base, with his or her back to the rest of the children, who stand at home. When "it" says "green light," all the children must run toward the base. When "it" says "red light," he or she turns around and all the children must stop right where they are. Any child who is caught moving after the "red light" must go back home and start over. The first child to reach the base is the next one who becomes "it."

What Else

To find out more interesting facts about the heart and lungs, consult *Blood and Guts* by Linda Allison. This book contains a wealth of information, including the fact that the average person's blood vessels, laid end to end, would stretch for sixty thousand miles!

While breathing rate and pulse rate are not the same, they are proportionately related since, when the heart pumps faster, the blood needs to pick up more oxygen from the lungs and the breathing rate increases. Refer the children to the chart they made during the hopscotch game to figure out how these two rates are related.

You might also want to institute a walking or running program. Make a chart to measure the group's progress. Do distances increase? Time periods shrink? Help the children set realistic goals for themselves.

To find out more about caring for the "airways," send a postcard to: The American Lung Association, 1740 Broadway, New York, NY 10019. Ask for "Information about How Lungs Work," "Air Pollution Information," and "Puzzles about Smoking and Air Pollution."

And finally, let the children take out those diagrams they've been so patiently working on and lay them over Figure 3-3. Invite the children to trace the heart, lungs, and major highways and airways with red felt-tipped pens. And there you have it: a picture of each child from the inside out!

COLLECTING CUT-UPS FROM THE FISH AND POULTRY STORE

Except for a searching stare into our mouths and throats, we're never really able to see the insides of our bodies. Or anyone else's, for that matter.

From a scientific point of view, the most interesting part of the body *is* the inside. And that's precisely what we *can't* see. A trip to the fish and poultry store can change all that, however, for a group of interested girls and boys. By examining the bones, joints, muscles, and organs of other animals, the children will easily relate that information to their own bodies. This systematic unveiling of the mysteries of the inner body should stimulate the children's curiosity, so that each dissection will be accompanied by lively questions, answers, and comments. (There's a lot to be said for the reverence of awestruck silence as well, however.)

Regardless of what the unique interest of each child is, dissecting souvenirs from the fish and poultry store will offer something special to all children. Direct experience with the otherwise hidden working parts of the body will expand the children's knowledge and appreciation of the human body. From this may come greater respect and care for their own bodies. How could anyone possibly surround their heart with fat or let those miraculous moving machines—the muscles—atrophy after examining these valuable gifts firsthand?

SETTING THE STAGE

Invite the children to discover the inner workings of their bodies:

Squeeze your arm from your shoulder all the way down to your fingertips. Can you find any bones? How many bones can you feel? If there are so many bones in just one arm, how do you suppose they all work together?

If you think your joints, muscles, and tendons are the helpers, you are right. But how do you suppose they work? And what about your heart or your stomach? You probably know where they are and what they do. But you could know so much more about these and other parts of your body if you could actually see and examine them!

As you can well imagine, seeing the inside of a person's body isn't the easiest thing to do. But by looking inside other animals that also have bones, joints, muscles, hearts, stomachs, and so forth, you can learn a lot about these parts in your own bodies.

WHAT TO DO BEFORE YOU GO

1. Review the charts from previous activities in this chapter so the children will be familiar with what goes where and how it works.
2. Make a list of the parts of the body the children would like to see. Write down everything that comes to mind even if you are not sure the fish and poultry shop will have it on hand.

3. Call the shopkeeper to see what is available. If this particular store does not have what you want, the shopkeeper can probably refer you to another place that does.

WHAT TO DO WHILE YOU'RE THERE

1. Take a good look around the shop. See how many items on your list you and the children can spot.
2. Ask the shopkeeper to wrap these items up for you. (Maybe you'd even like to find these parts firsthand: Order a *whole* fish or chicken to dissect!)
3. Show the list of remaining items to the shopkeeper and see how many of these things he can come up with.
4. Pay for your "specimens" and return to your "laboratory" for some serious dissecting.

WHAT TO DO AFTERWARD

1. Invite the children to carefully examine each item with their eyes and make a mental (or written) note of what they see.
2. Have the children gently, but purposefully, feel each item, touching it softly to discover the outer surface, then pressing firmly to feel what's inside. Note these things, too.
3. Speculate as to what's inside.
4. With a sharp knife, carefully cut into the specimen. Make large incisions in order to visualize as much of the insides as possible without having to "chop away" at them.
5. Have the children compare what is visible to what is on the charts they studied.
6. Write labels for each part you can identify, then have the children pin them on the appropriate parts.
7. Have the future surgeons draw pictures of what they see, either in booklet form or on a single wall chart.
8. Help the children try to find the parts in their own bodies that are similar to the parts of the animal's body you are examining.
9. Have the children make a list of what they are most interested in or have questions about. Take this list to the library or to a friend in the medical profession to continue the research.
10. Though the objects of your dissecting would not make a very appealing meal for people, these cut-ups may well delight a neighborhood cat or dog.

TAKE ME OUT TO THE BALL GAME

Sometimes it is just as important to introduce children to outings of special interest to *us* as it is to take them on outings of special interest to *them*. Appropriate "grownup" adventures are a way for us to share a facet of ourselves with our children. These outings can serve to develop an as yet undiscovered area of interest in our children and can also show the children firsthand that accommodating someone else's wishes can be great fun.

The psychological benefits to the children are many. They are initially flattered to be in on an outing that the grownup looks forward to, and are boosted by the opportunity to relate to the adult on an adult level. What's more, to see mom or dad so obviously having fun—and to be a part of it—provides a great lift to any child's self-esteem.

All of which takes us out to the ball game! What better way to share a sunny afternoon than to watch eighteen strong, healthy bodies at play? To see such physical fitness in action is surely an inspiring way to sum up the lessons of the previous activities in this chapter. And to be part of an event that is special to the mom or dad in attendance can make this day a major milestone in a child's summer.

SETTING THE STAGE
Invite the children to a very special outing:

> What has eighteen legs, nine heads, catches flies, and is fun to watch?
>
> Give up? A baseball team!
>
> And since a baseball team is so much fun to watch, I'm going to the baseball game. And I'm going to bring along someone very, very special.
>
> Can you guess who that very special someone is?
> It's *you!*

WHAT TO DO BEFORE YOU GO
1. Plan a good time to see the game. Afternoon games that are not doubleheaders are best. If there are no major league teams near you, how about a minor league or Little League game?
2. When you buy your tickets, consider the bleacher section. The price is much cheaper, the bleachers are frequently sunnier, the children will have more room to squirm, and you will be under fewer attacks by the souvenir and soda vendors. (If you worry that you may not see as well, bring binoculars.)
3. Explain the principles of baseball to the children, including how to score and who does what on each team. Talk about the team you'll be rooting for, and drop the names of favorite players you'll be watching.
4. If possible, play a game on your block before you go to give the children a better idea of how it is played.
5. Eat a hearty meal before you go or pack a picnic lunch to cut down on requests for snacks.
6. Have the children dress in "layers" so that they will be comfortable in both midday sun and late afternoon shade. And don't forget sunscreen for fair-skinned noses.
7. Sing a chorus of "Take Me Out to the Ball Game," and be on your way.

WHAT TO DO WHILE YOU'RE THERE
1. Before you get to your seat, point out the location of the nearest restroom to the children.
2. Enjoy! Share your enthusiasm with the children. *Don't* keep comments to yourself; rather, discuss the game as you would with any companion.
3. Answer questions as they arise. Point out spectacular plays. Call players by name.

WHAT TO DO WHEN YOU GET HOME
1. Make sure the child has someone to share the day with. Special outings take on their rosiest glow when the youngster has an interested dad or sister waiting to hear all about it.
2. Discuss the muscle development of the players. Which large muscles contribute to a good game? Which small muscles? What sort of heart–lung conditioning would be necessary? Why?
3. Try some batting practice and games of catch outside. If the interest level so dictates, set up your own program, noting specific skills and goals.

BOOKS FOR CONTINUING DISCOVERY

Books for Adults

ALLISON, LINDA. *Blood and Guts: A Working Guide to Your Own Insides.* Boston: Little, Brown, 1976.

BERSHAD, CAROL, and DEBORAH BERNICK. *Bodyworks.* New York: Random House, 1979.

LORIN, MARTIN I., M.D. *The Parents Book of Physical Fitness for Children.* New York: Atheneum, 1978.

RIGGS, MAIDA L. *Jump to Joy.* Englewood Cliffs, NJ: Prentice-Hall, 1980.

SCHNEIDER, TOM. *Everybody's a Winner.* Boston: Little, Brown, 1976.

SHAPIRO, LAWRENCE E. *Games to Grow On.* Englewood Cliffs, NJ: Prentice-Hall, 1981.

Books for Children

CARR, RACHEL. *Be a Frog, a Bird or a Tree.* New York: Harper Colophon Books, 1973.

KREMENTZ, JILL. *A Very Young Gymnast.* New York: Knopf, 1979.

WORSTELL, EMMA V. *Jump the Rope Jingles.* New York: Collier Books, 1969.

WYN, KAPIT, and LAWRENCE M. ELSON. *The Anatomy Coloring Book.* New York: Canfield Press, 1973.

CHAPTER FOUR

MUSIC

AN APPLE FROM THE TEACHER

Sound has a profound effect on our lives, and not just in the thoughts expressed in spoken words, or in the messages we receive from the wordless—but nevertheless meaningful—sounds of ambulance sirens, train whistles, and recess bells. The *quality* and *type* of sounds that communicate to us are as important as the message itself. Music celebrates this phenomenon beautifully and with infinite variety.

Without a word or any standardized means of encoding it, music can soothe an excited nervous system or stimulate a lazy one. And when it is created with expertise, music can take us through a guided tour of the solar system or even tell us what season it is. (Just listen to "The Planets" by Holst or "The Four Seasons" by Vivaldi.)

Music is fun. It makes us feel good inside. Sometimes the whole body enjoys music through dancing or exercising. And sometimes music makes our minds come alive even when our bodies are quiet. As children's participation in music develops from passive listening to organized songs and games, they will be gaining more than just an expanded repertoire of hits. Using songs they already know as models, they will create their own chorus line or solo performances. This is a great way for children to fill their leisure hours. And who knows? From this innocent play may come a special and long-lasting relationship with music.

The self-confidence that comes with achievement will encourage the boys and girls to explore higher and higher levels of music—whether it be as a patron or a performer. And while children hum, skip, vocalize, gesticulate, and pirouette to music, their overall development is making some important gains. On the most obvious level, children are learning to enjoy and appreciate music in new and interesting ways. However, they are also developing mind–body coordination, from which they will reap many benefits ranging from orderly thinking to fluid and creative self-expression.

All this, from the joy of music.

PUT ON YOUR LISTENING EARS

Along with a friendly smile or a handshake, music can be interpreted as a universal language. Music can soften or enliven the atmosphere, or it may spark wild fantasies of faraway places. What makes this so very special is that the common denominator of each musical creation is not necessarily a trained musician.

Everyone enjoys music, whether through active participation or by passively listening to a favorite recording. "Put On Your Listening Ears" brings to life that seed of musicianship that lies within each of us. For the child, this first involves the basic aspects of music: sound and rhythm. Activities in this area also prepare the child for reading by developing auditory discrimination and memory. Children will train their ears to appreciate a variety of musical sounds that will bring increasing pleasure for each child and, perhaps, inspire a new hobby as well.

SETTING THE STAGE
Invite the child to reconsider familiar sounds and possibly discover some new ones:

Can you name some of the sounds you hear every day? Listen to those sounds in your mind. Think of your favorite sound. Listen carefully . . .

Now listen to water in a swimming pool just after you've jumped in. Listen to a train speeding down the track. What about chimes moving in the wind? Or a drum in a marching band?

What do you hear when you listen to these sounds? How do they make you feel? If you wanted to play some music, which sounds would you want to make?

If you use your imagination and good listening ears you can discover a lot about sounds and music.

WHAT YOU'LL NEED
1. 2 chairs
2. Small blanket
3. Large drinking glass
4. Pencil
5. 2 small pieces of wood or sticks
6. 2 butter knives
7. Bowl of water
8. Several sheets of paper

HOW TO DO IT
1. Place the chairs 3 or 4 feet apart and drape the blanket over them to make a curtain. Place the remaining materials on one side of the curtain and have the children sit on the other side so they can't see the objects.
2. Show the children each "instrument" and the sound it makes (tap the glass with the pencil, tap the sticks together, lightly tap the knives together, splash the water with your hand, and crumple a sheet of paper).
3. Place the instruments behind the curtain so the children can't see them.
4. Go behind the curtain and play first a single "instrument" and then a series of them; have the children identify the sounds they hear.

What Else

Now that the children have identified obvious differences in sounds and sequence, try adding rhythm as another variable in the exercise. You can also refine the child's listening skills by using one "instrument" for a variety of volume and tonal qualities. For example, you could use several glasses, each filled with a different amount of water. This increased awareness will necessarily improve the child's appreciation of music.

The next step is to play a variety of music—classical, marches, rock—and ask the child to identify the sounds and feeling that come with hearing the music. The children can even play or sing along with the music.

Of course, all this wonderful creativity should be recognized, so why not start your own tape library of the favorite music of you and the children? And don't forget the children's new composition!

LET YOUR FINGERS DO THE SINGING

If you've been fretting over otherwise chatty children who suddenly become mute whenever they are invited to participate in any kind of musical activity, here's just what you need to add musical pleasure to your life and theirs: fingerplays (songs that may be acted out with the hands as well as sung with the voice) are perfect for the young musicians two or three years old as well as for the more mature and accomplished child who has well-developed memory and motor control. The toddler can "sing" a song by just imitating a few hand motions. This lays a strong foundation for developing mind–body coordination and a sense of rhythm. And in the midst of all this movement and melody, the children are easily charmed into extending their attention spans.

Initially, all that may be required of the child is a single motion with the hand. Each performance (either in a group or alone) is pressure free and lots of fun. This innocent play builds confidence in the child which, of course, is a real asset. This is also an expert way to channel excess energy which might prevent a child from sitting and listening. This is a definite plus for adults, too!

SETTING THE STAGE
Invite the children to sing with their hands:

> What if your older brother loved to sing and he sang to you every day? One day he woke up with laryngitis, but he still wanted to sing to you.
>
> So what did he do?
>
> He sang one song by making circles with his hands, and another by folding his arms in front of himself and rocking them back and forth, and another by making a fist with his thumb sticking out like a tail. Can you imagine what those songs were about?
>
> There are lots of songs you can sing with your hands even if you don't have laryngitis. In fact, using your hands makes it more fun, and you don't even have to remember all the words if you don't want to!

WHAT YOU'LL NEED
1. You, the children, and a quiet, comfortable place to sit together

HOW TO DO IT
Chant or sing the following words (make up your own melody) as you perform the hand movements noted in parentheses):

Circle Song

Round is a pancake	(Fingertips of both hands touch each other to form a circle.)
Round is a plum	(Repeat motion.)

Round is a doughnut	(Extend arms in front of you to form a circle.)
Round is a drum	(Pretend to play a drum.)
Rat-ta-ta-tat, Rat-ta-ta-tat, Rat-ta-ta-tat-tat-tat.	(Repeat motion.)
Round is a puppy curled up on a rug	(Draw arms close to body.)
Round are the spots on a wee ladybug.	(Make tiny circle with fingers.)
Look all round you	(Point around room.)
On the ground	(Point down.)
And in the air	(Point up.)
And you can find round things everywhere.	(Make circle with hands.)

The Turtle Song (Words by Vachel Lindsay):

There was a little turtle	(Make a fist with thumb sticking out.)
Who lived in a box	(Trace square in air.)
He swam in the puddles	(Move turtle in air.)
And climbed on the rocks.	(Turtle moves onto fist of other hand.)
He snapped at the mosquito	(Hand opens and shuts.)
He snapped at the flea	(Repeat motion.)
He snapped at the minnow	(Repeat motion.)
And he snapped at me.	(Repeat motion.)
He caught the mosquito	(Repeat motion.)
He caught the flea	(Repeat motion.)
He caught the minnow	(Repeat motion.)
But he didn't catch me!	(Wave index finger.)

Mr. Wally (Miss Molly) — (Can be acted out with two children:

Mr. Wally had a dolly who was sick, sick, sick.	(Rock dolly in arms.)
So he called for the doctor to come quick, quick, quick.	(Dial telephone.)
The doctor came with her bag	(Hold bag in front of you.)
And her hat,	(Pat head.)
She knocked on the door	(Knock on door)
With a rat-ta-tat-tat.	(Repeat motion.)
She looked at the dolly and she shook her head.	(Shake head.)

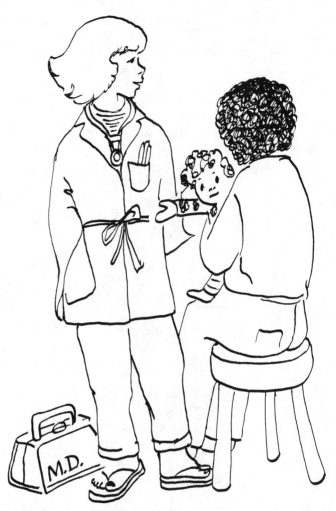

Mr. Wally, put your dolly straight
  to bed.   (Point index finger.)
She wrote on a paper for some
  pills, pills, pills   (Write.)
I'll be back in the morning with my
  bill, bill, bill.   (Wave.)

What Else

Introduce the word *pantomime* to the children and then do a fingerplay
with actions only. You can have one child pantomime a song and have
the other children guess what it is.

You can also extend each fingerplay by discussing what you sang about. For example, you can look for round things in the environment after doing the "Circle Song," or ask the children what is the best thing to do when they are sick, or ask, "What in the world is a minnow?"

Finally, the children may be inspired to make up their own fingerplays to favorite songs. They might also enjoy the wealth of fingerplays contained in *Eye Winker, Tom Tinker, Chin Chopper* by Tom Glazer.

LISTENING WITH YOUR BODY

A catchy tune is often referred to as a "real toe-tapper." Sometimes we are so absorbed in the music we're listening to that our entire body responds with some sort of rhythmical movement.

Spontaneous movement exploration is a great way to improve mind–body coordination with a touch of individual creativity. "Listening with Your Body" develops the ability to enjoy music actively, rather than passively. Initially, this response is improvisational. But this spontaneity can give rise to the child's systematically developing original dance routines.

The spontaneity of this activity shows children that anything is possible in music. Guided by their own creative resources, they can become choreographers. Whether it is planned or entirely spontaneous, this physical activity has a wonderfully healthful effect on the body by toning muscles and developing coordination. And the mind that guides a healthy, active body becomes one that is confident, relaxed, clear, and often exhilarated. Music beautifully enhances this process.

SETTING THE STAGE
Invite the children to discover how effortless it is to listen to music with their bodies:

> What if you had to take a nap and the local high school marching band decided to practice in the empty lot across from your house. You're sleepy enough to go to sleep, but you don't.

> Your body just can't seem to settle down. Without even doing it on purpose, you realize you are tapping your foot or head or hand (or maybe all three) in time with the music.

> Although you are not taking your nap, you are discovering something very important about listening to music. Music affects your whole body! So the next time you listen to some really neat music, let yourself go and let your body play the same way you hear the music being played.

WHAT YOU'LL NEED
1. A large open area (at least 10 by 10 feet)
2. Phonograph or tape player
3. A variety of instrumental music, such as "La Mer" by Debussy, "Appalachian Spring" by Aaron Copeland, or "Bellavia" by Chuck Mangione

HOW TO DO IT
1. Play a musical recording that has a distinctive style or feeling to it.
2. Spend a moment or two with the children just listening to the music.
3. Begin to move your body or parts of your body in time to the music. Invite the children to do the same. When the children have become caught up in the music, remove yourself from the picture and the children will become even less inhibited than before.

What Else

Children will become more and more comfortable with this process with practice. As this happens, you may give the children a prop (a maraca, a scarf, a feather duster) to enhance their routines.

Some guidelines might set new creative juices flowing, too. Give directions, such as: "Move only your arms," "Hold the prop with your teeth," "Tie the scarf around your legs." You can also have the children try "mirror-image" dancing with partners. Or how about mood dances, where the body expresses various moods?

DRAW A SONG

Drawing to music allows the child to respond to music in a new way, thereby enlivening another facet of individual creativity. This process creates new images in the child's awareness which, in turn, give new meaning, appreciation, and enjoyment to music. Abstract feelings and thoughts that arise when we listen to music somehow become more concrete when they are put on paper, even if it is through abstract drawing. (Haven't you ever felt like a wavy line or a burst of color at one time or another?) The process of drawing to music also shows the child how the arts are integrated.

SETTING THE STAGE
Invite the child to respond to music in yet another way:

> You can listen to a song. Write words to a song. Write notes to a song. Record a song. Sing a song. Dance to a song. But how in the world would you draw a song?

WHAT YOU'LL NEED
1. A large piece of paper for each child. A long roll of shelf or butcher paper works best.
2. A variety of drawing tools, such as pens, pencils, crayons, and pastels.
3. Record or tape player.
4. Some really good, evocative music. ("The Planets" by Holst or "LaMer" by Debussy are good for this exercise and can probably be borrowed from your public library.)

HOW TO DO IT
1. Have the youngsters sit quietly in front of the paper for a few moments.
2. Begin the music.
3. Let the children draw whatever comes to mind, whether it is a concrete thought or an abstract feeling.

What Else

Whatever medium the child chooses, spontaneity and introspective listening are the key in this activity. For something different, you may want to use chalk on a sidewalk that needs decorating. Then, after each song, the children can share their drawings. This display will easily show the children how different people interpret the same thing in different ways.

After the children have had some practice, you can discuss in depth what they've drawn. Let the youngsters tell you how they felt and

what they thought of when they made their drawings. For instance, if a girl drew soft, wavy lines while listening to "LaMer," Debussy's feelings about the ocean were understood. Imagine the excitement that child will feel when she discovers she has "communicated" with a famous composer!

MAKE YOUR OWN MUSIC

One of the truly glorious things about music is that it is so open-ended. The variety of form and style in music is virtually endless. And so are the instruments with which that music is played. (There is a rumor on the West Coast that the only "instrument" that the rather unorthodox Stanford University marching band has *not* played is a bird cage!)

Any child with a song in his or her heart can become a virtuoso with a few household discards and a touch of creativity. Here's how.

SETTING THE STAGE
Invite the children to design and make their "own kind of music."

How many musical instruments can you name?

Did you think of a glass of water? Or a pie plate? Or some wood? What makes you think these are *not* musical instruments?

You have probably never heard a musical group that featured pie plates and a glass of water. But in the same way that there are lots of ways to play an instrument, there are lots of ways to *make* instruments. Just put your imagination to work!

Drum

WHAT YOU'LL NEED
1. Empty oatmeal box with lid
2. Tape
3. Paste
4. Construction paper
5. Scissors
6. Spoons for drumsticks

HOW TO DO IT
1. Help the children tape the lid to the box.
2. Let the children cut and paste various construction paper designs on the "drum."
3. To play the "drum," simply beat on it with the spoons.

Maraca

WHAT YOU'LL NEED
1. Empty paper towel or bathroom tissue roll
2. Tape
3. Heavy paper
4. Several dry beans
5. ¼ cup glue and ¼ cup water mixed together
6. Colored tissue paper torn into small pieces

HOW TO DO IT
1. Help the children tape a piece of heavy paper securely over one end of the roll.
2. Put the beans inside the roll and seal the other end securely with the heavy paper.
3. Have the children dip the tissue paper into the glue solution and cover all sides of the roll with 3 or 4 layers of paper.
4. Let the maraca dry thoroughly for a few days before using. It should be very hard.
5. The maraca is played by shaking it in time to the beat of a favorite song.

Cymbals

WHAT YOU'LL NEED
1. 2 tin pie plates
2. Super-strength glue that will adhere wood to metal
3. 2 large wooden beads or blocks

HOW TO DO IT

1. Glue the bead or block to the center of the outside bottom of each pie plate. Be careful to use the glue according to the directions on the package, and let it dry overnight.
2. Hold the cymbals by the wooden handles and clap them together to punctuate a rousing tune.

Water Chimes

WHAT YOU'LL NEED

1. Five drinking glasses (made of real glass)
2. Tap water
3. Pencil

HOW TO DO IT

1. Fill four of the glasses ¼, ½, ¾, and completely full, respectively. Leave the fifth glass empty.
2. Tap each glass lightly with the pencil and have the boys and girls note the differences in sound.
3. Now invite the children to create a tune.

Rhythm Blocks

WHAT YOU'LL NEED

1. Four wooden blocks, preferably the same size, that are small enough so that a child can hold one in one hand
2. Enough sandpaper to cover one side of two blocks
3. Scissors
4. Glue

HOW TO DO IT

1. Help the children cut the sandpaper so it will completely cover the side of one block. Cut another piece the same size.
2. Have the children glue one piece of sandpaper on each of two blocks.
3. To play the rhythm blocks, strike them together or rub them against each other. Play the blocks without sandpaper the same way as the blocks with sandpaper.

What Else

With just these few instruments, the children have enough to create all kinds of music. The instruments can be used for solo performances or in a well-organized orchestration. (Improvised "jazz" concerts are great, too!) The boys and girls can use their instruments to accompany a favorite recording or a "real" instrument such as a piano or guitar.

Another aspect of making your own kind of music would be to select several of the children's favorites and then record them on one tape that can be used during special times, such as quiet time or even travel time, if you happen to have a tape player in your car.

And finally, apart from their obvious musical uses, these instruments are excellent tools for developing and refining eye–hand coordination in children.

HEY, KIDS! LET'S PUT ON A SHOW!

With the first smiles infants show the world at large, they come to know the vast joy and rewards that come with performing. Innocent, fun-filled exhibitions of talent (walking across the room alone, speaking a sentence, catching a ball) reinforce a particular skill by supporting the child with the knowledge that he or she is capable of great accomplishment. As children mature and gain more sophisticated skills such as singing, dancing, or playing a musical instrument, their ability to share these talents grows accordingly.

Staging a show can involve talents ranging from a toddler doing the hand motions to "Twinkle, Twinkle, Little Star" to a grade school child leading a discussion on musical analysis. This culmination of their talents provides a great boost to their level of self-confidence and gives rise to a lively spirit of cooperation and creativity.

Young children thrive on being able to perform, whether it is for friends and family or an attentive group of favorite dolls and stuffed animals. Inhibitions that often plague older children (and many adults) melt away in favor of an effortless display of individual talents.

SETTING THE STAGE
Invite a group of children to explore their talents and find ways of sharing them with others:

Think of something you know how to do really well, something that is so great that other people would enjoy watching or listening to you do it.

You've probably seen people on television who are really good at singing or playing an instrument. They wear fancy clothes and put on a show for all the people who want to see them. They always look like they are having so much fun.

Imagine how exciting it would be to have people watch *you* perform and clap for *you* when you were done. Then you would be a real star, just like those people you saw on TV!

WHAT YOU'LL NEED
1. Several sheets of writing paper
2. Pens or pencils

3. Props (as needed for specific acts)
4. Several sheets of construction paper
5. Felt pens
6. Paste
7. Scissors

HOW TO DO IT

1. Invite the children to take stock of their talents and plan how they would like to perform. Perhaps someone would like to read a favorite poem or sing an original song. Maybe another child could tap dance or twirl a baton. Let imaginations run wild. (At this stage in their careers, a "variety show" format is much easier for the children to work with than a dramatic production.)
2. List all of the children who want to participate in the show and note what each wants to do.
3. On a separate sheet of paper for each child, write down that child's name and the nature of his or her performance.
4. Select a Master of Ceremonies (preferably someone who can read), and discuss the responsibilities of that job.
5. Meet with each child individually to discuss what preparation will be needed for the performance. On that child's sheet, list any props or other special directions that are necessary to make that act a success.
6. Meet with the whole group again to decide on an order to the program, and the date, time, and place of the performance.
7. Use construction paper, pens, paste, and scissors to make posters or individual invitations announcing the performance. You may also wish to write out some programs to hand out at the show.
8. Rehearse until the children are comfortable with their numbers.
9. On the day of the performance, briefly go over everyone's acts, then . . . on with the show!

What Else

The children have just accomplished a great feat. They have developed talents and proceeded with confidence to work together to successfully entertain others. This calls for a celebration! Plan a cast party for all the players and their patrons complete with festive food, decorations (including posters from the performance, of course), and maybe even an encore or two!

A VISIT TO THE MUSIC STORE

Thanks to modern technology, children, regardless of their age or where they live, are able to listen to any kind of music produced by any kind of instrument any place in the world. Even synthetic music is commonplace.

Children's understanding and appreciation of music may be sophisticated, but what has their actual experiences with music been? They know a lot of creative and entertaining things to do with music, but they might not know how the music they hear is made. A visit to the music store will put the child in touch with the source of music: the musical instrument itself.

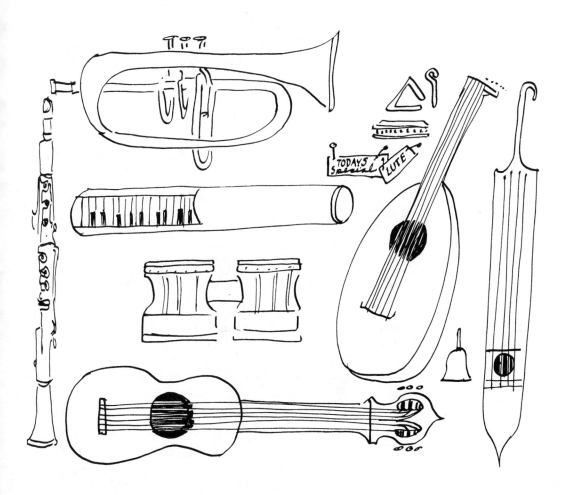

A visit to the music store gives children concrete experience with the "tools of the trade" they have been working with thus far. While they may sound similar to the children, once the boys and girls have seen and experimented with a trumpet and a French horn, each instrument's uniqueness will be forever emblazoned on their minds. The next time a child hears those instruments played, it will be like hearing from an old friend. And who knows? This experience may easily give rise to more fun with music, from increasing the child's appreciation to developing a new hobby.

SETTING THE STAGE

Invite the child to consider all the ways in which music can be made:

If you wanted to make some music, what would you do? You know how to use things around your house like oatmeal boxes and pie plates to make music, so maybe you would use these.

But if you want the challenge and fun of something a little different, you might want to explore the instruments other musicians use. You can see and touch them and probably even try your hand at playing them just by making a visit to the music store!

WHAT TO DO BEFORE YOU GO

1. Play some records featuring a variety of music. Soloists or small group ensembles are best. "Fanfare for the Common Man" by Copeland, "Toccata in D" by Bach, or "Peter and the Wolf" by Prokofiev are good selections.
2. Indentify the instruments you hear and have the children make a list of them.
3. Phone your local music store. Let them know your plans, and arrange for a convenient time to visit.

WHAT TO DO WHEN YOU'RE THERE

1. Make a brief tour of the store on your own before meeting the clerk, making mental notes of interesting and unusual sights and sounds. Notice which instruments the children are most intrigued by. You can ask about all this later.
2. Introduce yourself and the children to the clerk who will show you the music store, and then let this person take over. (Most music stores welcome young visitors and will know exactly how to conduct the tour.)
3. Try to have the children experiment—carefully, of course—with some of the instruments, especially the ones on their list. Invite the children to ask whatever questions they might have.
4. The music store will probably have a bulletin board posting times and dates of various recitals and/or youth symphonies. If possible, arrange to take the children to one of these exciting events.

WHAT TO DO AFTERWARD

1. Discuss the events of the day. Older children might enjoy discussing different categories of instruments and how they evolved from ancient instruments. (This, in fact, is the making of a fine research project.)
2. Play the same music you listened to before going to the music store and see what new sounds you can identify.
3. Invite a musician to play for you (this can be a big brother who plays the violin or a mom who plays the clarinet). Perhaps after the concert, the children can try their hands at playing that instrument.

BAND PRACTICE FROM THE SIDELINES

The following field trip is a way for both you and the child to learn from behind the scenes what it takes to put on a fancy half time show. What's more, this may be the child's only opportunity to see a real live band. By seeing the details of the performance being worked out firsthand, the children will get ideas on how to work out their own routines. But most of all, seeing band practice from the sidelines will be lots of fun.

SETTING THE STAGE

Invite the children behind the scenes:

If you've ever watched a marching band on TV, I'm sure you love listening to the exciting music. But I'll bet you were even more impressed by the fancy designs the band members made with their bodies while they played their instruments.

What do you think it takes to make those routines work out so perfectly every time? If you said practice—and more practice—you're not only right, but that's a hint as to where we're going today.

WHAT TO DO BEFORE YOU GO

1. Phone the music department of your local high school or college. Ask for the director of the marching band.
2. Explain your situation to the director. Ask if it would be possible to have a small group of well-behaved aspiring band members watch their rehearsal. Arrange for a convenient time to visit.
3. Arrange transportation for your field trip. Now may be an excellent time to explore the advantages of public transportation.

WHAT TO DO WHILE YOU'RE THERE

1. Watch and listen attentively and enjoy the show. If there are bleachers, sit high up for the best view.

2. Give special attention to how the rehearsal is run. Do the band members try certain phases of the routine over and over again? Make sure this aspect of "practice makes perfect" is not lost on the children.
3. The band director and its members probably have busy school schedules before and after practice, so your visit may be limited to watching from the sidelines. But if the opportunity presents itself, introduce yourself and the children to a few of the performers.

WHAT TO DO AFTERWARD
1. Recount the events of the outing by way of discussion, highlighting any new and interesting things the girls and boys saw.
2. Discuss in what ways the children's performances are similar to or different from the "big time" band you just saw.
3. Now that they have seen a band practice, have the children plan a new marching routine they can perform at the next dodgeball game on the block. (Who knows? You may end up with the youngest marching band ensemble at your town's next Fourth of July parade!)
4. Have the children draw pictures of what they liked most about what they saw.
5. Write individual or group "thank you" notes to the director of the band and its members. (The children's drawings from the previous step will make delightful stationery.)
6. Mark off a course on your driveway or playyard with chalk and have the children march on this design. Accompany the march with music from an obligingly loud stereo, a portable cassette player, or instruments the children can play as they march.

BOOKS FOR CONTINUING DISCOVERY

Books for Adults

FOWKE, EDITH. *Sally Go Round the Sun.* New York: Doubleday, 1978.

GLAZER, TOM. *Eye Winker, Tom Tinker, Chin Chopper.* New York: Doubleday, 1973.

LANGSTAFF, NANCY AND JOHN. *Jim Along Josie.* New York: Harcourt Brace Jovanovich, Inc., 1970.

PECK, JUDITH. *Leap to the Sun.* Englewood Cliffs, N.J.: Prentice-Hall, 1980.

RITCHIE, JEAN. *Folk Songs of the Southern Appalachians.* New York: Oak Publications, 1965.

WINN, MARIE. *Fireside Book of Children's Songs.* New York: Simon & Schuster, 1966.

Books for Children

KREMENTZ, JILL. *The Very Young Dancer.* New York: Knopf, 1976.

Records

"Big Bird Leads the Band," CTW Sesame Street, Sesame Street Records.

"Peter and the Wolf" by Prokofiev, performed by The Vienna Philharmonic with Hermione Gingold, conducted by Karl Böhm, Deutsche Grammophon.

CHAPTER FIVE

MATHEMATICS

AN APPLE FROM THE TEACHER

Math is a subject with many bonuses. The obvious benefit is that children learn to count and perform other useful mathematical operations, which are handy skills in anyone's life. The systematic thought process inherent to any mathematical function does more than just solve a number problem, however. Working with mathematical equations trains the mind to think in an orderly and logical manner. This asset is appreciated long after the student leaves the math class.

In this chapter, manipulative materials are used to give the child a head start in the math department by offering the youngster concrete experience with abstract concepts. By using these materials, a five-year-old child can confidently solve many numerical operations. This method of exploring mathematics handily alleviates the possibility of panic a child may experience when, looking at the number 171, the question is posed, "which '1' is greater?" If he or she is holding a unit bead in one hand and a hundred square in the other, the child can clearly see that the "1's" in the number 171 stand for very different quantities.

In addition to manipulative materials, this chapter uses math games to teach mathematical concepts. These games translate spontaneous play into an enjoyable training program that offers the children important mathematical knowledge and fosters orderly, purposeful thinking.

IS 5 MORE THAN 10?

Tiny children seem to come into the world with numerical foreknowledge. It is not uncommon to find children who are 2½ years old blissfully counting to themselves while at play. Actually, this is usually the result of a well-meaning adult's labor. Teaching a child to count without the benefit of manipulative materials *is* good for the child: It is a great auditory memory exercise that unfortunately has nothing to do with practical mathematical knowledge. However, a solid basis for all work in the decimal system can easily be formed with the use of simple, well-ordered counting games similar to the ones that follow.

SETTING THE STAGE

Invite the child to consider the importance of learning to count:

If you ever have a party and want to make your drinks really fancy, put small pieces of fruit in each space in your ice-cube tray along with the water before you put the tray back into the freezer.

This sounds simple enough. But how many pieces of fruit should you slice? If you have too many, you'll have wasted fruit. If you don't have enough, you'll be stuck with plain ice cubes.

But this will be no problem for you if you know how to count. So before you make these fancy ice cubes or do *anything* that involves counting, you'd better do some practicing.

WHAT YOU'LL NEED
1. 10 pieces of white railroad board, each 10 by 4 inches
2. Heavy-duty hole punch
3. 10 8-inch shoelaces
4. 55 ½-inch beads, all the same size and color
5. A basket large enough to hold the beads
6. A tray large enough to hold the bead basket and the white cards
7. Felt pen the same color as the beads

HOW TO DO IT
1. Place each card lengthwise in front of you. Number them 1 through 10. Put the number on the left side of the card.

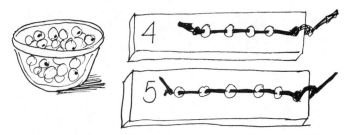

2. Punch a hole in the middle of the right side of the card, about ½ inch from the edge.
3. Tie one end of the shoelace through the hole.
4. Stack the cards on the tray along with the basket containing the beads.
5. Have each child take a turn choosing a card, reading the number on it, and stringing that number of beads on the shoelace.
6. Continue the game until all the children have had a turn and all the beads have been counted.
7. So that the children can check their own work, you may want to draw the correct number of beads on the back of each card with the felt pen.

What Else

Make a mystery bag counting game with numerals written on individual pieces of paper in one bag and fifty-five small objects in another bag. Have the child reach in the first bag, get a numeral, and then reach into the second bag and pull out the appropriate number of objects.

Older children can get practice by playing dominoes or "math lotto": To make the lotto cards, mark off nine 1-inch squares across the top and down the side of pieces of tagboard. Draw lines to make 81 squares, then in each square put various numbers of stickers (or simply colored circles) representing numbers from 1 to 9. Write the numerals 1 through 9 on individual 3-by-5-inch cards. To play the game, the children each take a playing card, then take turns drawing a numeral card. The children may mark off (with pennies or other small tokens) those squares that contain the same number of stickers as the numerals on the drawn card. The first child to fill up a line of nine on an individual playing card wins. (When making the cards, be sure to place the stickers in a random arrangement.)

Finally, reinforce basic counting skills as you read *Brian Wildsmith's 1,2,3* and *Numbers* by John J. Reiss. You may also read (or sing, if the children know the tune) *Over in the Meadow* by Ezra Jack Keats.

(Note: Once the children have mastered the counting concepts, you can use the original materials and the mystery bag as aids in teaching introductory addition and subtraction.)

WHOSE PLACE IS IT ANYHOW?

The following Montessori-inspired activity lays out a simple yet highly effective technique for teaching the fundamentals of the decimal system to young children. The approach is multisensory, and the results are marvelous. Within a short time, the child should intuitively grasp the difference between *ones, tens,* and *hundreds.* It will become quite evident, for perhaps the first time, that the "1" in the number 15 represents far more than the "5." This basic understanding has obvious, as well as academic, applications:

The child's chances for success with dynamic mathematical operations are greatly improved when they are done within a framework of this sort. For example, 356 becomes more than a series of digits. What's more, making sense out of dollars and dimes and, later, using metric measurement systems, become easy progressions from this simple and basic exercise.

By the way, the materials the children will make in the latter part of this activity serve as more than conceptual reinforcement. They will be put to happy use in "The Bank Game" that follows.

SETTING THE STAGE
Invite the child to notice different number values:

Which do you think is more? The number 5 or 15?

That was easy. The number 15 is certainly more than 5. But here's a harder question to think about.

Which *numeral* in fifteen stands for more—the 1 or the 5?

If you said "1," you're right. But do you know why?

The 5 is in the *ones* place, so it stands for five ones, or 5. The 1 is in the *tens* place, so it stands for one ten, or 10.

It may sound confusing, but it's actually quite simple, once you find out whose place a numeral is in! Let's try.

WHAT YOU'LL NEED
1. Posterboard
2. Scissors
3. Felt pen
4. Ruler
5. Construction paper
6. Paste

HOW TO DO IT
1. To make your visual aids:
    - Cut a piece of posterboard that is 1 by 1 inch. This is your *one unit.*

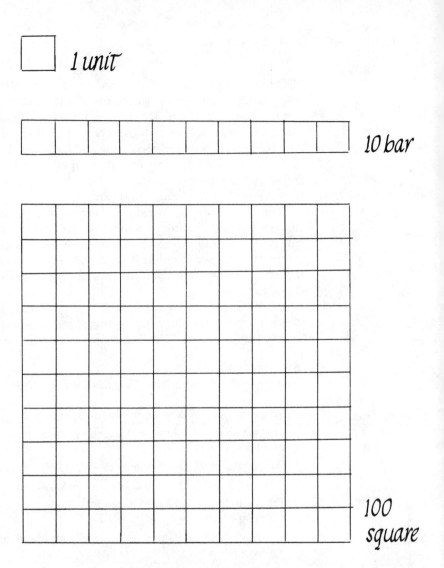

1 unit

10 bar

100 square

- Cut a piece of posterboard that is equal to 10 *one units* laid end to end. Mark off the units. This is your *ten bar*.
- Cut a piece of posterboard that is equal to 10 *ten bars* laid side by side to form a square. Again, mark off the units. This is your *hundred square*.

2. Present these place markers to the children one at a time in this manner: Show them the one unit. Say "This is 1." Let each of the children take turns holding it and saying what it is. Remove it, and present the ten bar in the same fashion. Do the same with the hundred square.

3. Bring out the three place markers together. Let the children experience the differences between the three on a visual and a tactile level.

4. Quiz the children. Take turns asking each one to point out 1 or 10 or 100.

5. Once the children have mastered the identification process, let them count the number of units within each of the pieces.

6. Let the children make their own one units, ten bars, and hundred squares. Pass out pieces of construction paper on which all the one units have been outlined. Have the children cut out the individual one units. Then have them paste these units on black sheets that are the size of either ten bars or hundred squares. (Save them for "The Bank Game," which follows.)

What Else

To relate the activity back to the number 15 presented earlier, simply line up 5 one units end to end beside 1 ten bar. The children will easily see that 1 ten is indeed greater than 5 ones.

Then explain that number places always progress, smallest to largest, from right to left. Line up the one unit, one ten bar, and one hundred square in this fashion to reinforce your explanation.

To make visuals of a more permanent nature, use colored wooden or metal beads. The one unit is 1 bead. The ten bar is 10 beads wired together to form a bar. The hundred square is 10 ten bars wired together to make a flat square. And to make a thousand cube, simply stack 10 hundred squares one atop the other, and wire them together!

THE BANK GAME

The previous activity provided the children with basic knowledge of our decimal system. "The Bank Game" gives these young mathematicians an opportunity to put this knowledge to use in fun and creative play.

"The Bank Game," another Montessori inspiration, reinforces the principles of place value by allowing the youngster to physically manipulate the place markers. It also gives the child a concrete understanding of the relationship between numbers and quantity.

Finally, the following activity gives children a chance to do some role playing of definite practical value. Once the children understand the simple parameters of the game, they can make up their own situations. The variations are endless.

SETTING THE STAGE

Invite the children to put theoretical knowledge of the decimal system to practical use:

Do you ever go shopping with your mom or dad? Have you ever picked out a package of cookies, only to hear, "That costs too much money!"

The question is, how do you *know* it costs too much money? How do you know that something with "111" stamped on it costs more than something with "89"?

Once again, it all has to do with places. We're going to play a game now called "The Bank Game," which will show you exactly why 111 is more than 89. We'll use the one units, ten bars, and hundred squares we just made.

WHAT YOU'LL NEED

1. A collection of place markers—about 9 of each for each child—from the previous activity. If you run short, use blank paper cut in the appropriate size and shape.
2. A large tray
3. A paper plate for each child
4. Paper
5. Pencils

HOW TO DO IT

1. Before you begin the game, review the lesson from the previous activity, adding this new information: Write the number 356 very large on a sheet of paper. As you point to each digit, say "Three hundreds, five tens, six ones." Then place the appropriate number of place markers on each digit. Do this with several numbers until all the children catch on.
2. Select the child with the best grasp of place value to be the first "banker." You be the "boss."
3. Arrange the place markers in order on a large tray in front of the banker.
4. Give each child a paper plate.
5. Send each child in turn to the banker for "money." Write on a slip of paper the amount, such as 356, that you'd like the child to "withdraw." The child then presents the slip to the banker, who places the appropriate number of place markers on the child's paper plate. The child then returns to you and counts out the "money" for you. If it is correct, you can send the youngster back to the banker to make a "deposit."
6. When the children have a good grasp of the game, they can take turns being the boss as well as the banker. You can seize this opportunity to withdraw to a quiet corner with a good book!

What Else

Let the children vary the game any way they want. They can set up a toy store, supermarket, or restaurant, for example, where they can spend the money they just withdrew. Just remind the young entrepreneurs to make regular deposits to keep enough money in circulation!

At some point during the game, be sure to relate the visual to the verbal. That is, be sure each child recognizes that "three hundreds, five tens, and six ones" are equal to 356 as well as to "3 hundred markers, 5 ten bars, and 6 one units." If there is any confusion, let the children total the individual units in the place markers to a certain number. (A number considerably smaller than 356 might be more practical at this stage!)

If the time is right and the level of interest is high, by all means take this opportunity to introduce the children to monetary values. Set out one of each of the place markers in a row, then place a penny, dime, and dollar on top of the appropriate marker and go from there!

Finally, if you happen to have an abacus on hand, let the older children explore this age-old Oriental calculator.

IS IT TOMORROW YET?

Anticipation most assuredly adds to excitement, especially for children. Yet as any parent can glumly tell you, the child's added excitement is far outweighed by the tedium of explaining over and over to the expectant child, "This is not the day of your party. It is the day after tomorrow."

What can best allow the thrill of anticipation while minimizing the agony of impatience? The answer is simplicity itself:

A calendar.

Obviously, the magical appearance of the calendar on the child's wall is not enough to do the trick. First, the child must have some preliminary understanding of "yesterday, today, and tomorrow." And, second, the youngster must somehow be involved directly with the calendar itself.

These things accomplished, however—as they will be in the activity to come—the child will find waiting for special days much easier. More importantly, the marking of time will be happily demystified for the child. Making plans and organizing time will become possible. And the child will grow in self-sufficiency in yet another direction.

SETTING THE STAGE

Invite the boys and girls to consider the utility of the calendar:

124

Think back to your last birthday. Did you have a party? Did you send out invitations to some special people?

You were probably so excited that the first thing you asked your mom or dad every morning was, "Is my party today?" I'll bet you thought it was *never* going to come!

One way to find out when a special day is going to come is to look on a calendar. A calendar is a chart that has a space for every day in each month. By looking at a calendar, you can easily tell which day is today, which was yesterday, and which is tomorrow. By looking at a calendar, in fact, you can even *count* the number of days between today and that special birthday party, so that when you first jump out of bed, you can run to your calendar and know that today isn't the party day . . . but tomorrow is!

And all of a sudden, waiting won't be so hard.

WHAT YOU'LL NEED
1. 3 lengths of adding machine tape, about 4 feet long each
2. Masking tape
3. Colored pens or pencils
4. Posterboard, at least 15 by 20 inches for each calendar, which can be a group calendar or a personal one for each child
5. Ruler
6. Black felt-tipped pen

HOW TO DO IT
1. Your first task is to familiarize the children with the ephemeral relationship between yesterday, today, and tomorrow. Here's how:
   - Hang a length of adding machine tape vertically on the wall. Call it "Today." Measure off blocks to represent regular intervals of time. As each interval draws to a close, draw a picture to represent the major activity during that time slot.
   - Hang a blank length of tape next to "Today." Call it "Tomorrow."
   - The next day, point to the "Today" tape and say, "This is 'Yesterday.' " Point to the "Tomorrow" tape and say, "This is now 'Today.' " Fill it in as you did before.
   - Hang up the third length of tape and, again, call it "Tomorrow."
2. The children have probably grasped the concept by now. Nonetheless, they may still enjoy making "time lines" every day. They can also use the "Tomorrow" tape as a planner.
3. Once the yesterday–today–tomorrow concept has been mastered, begin on the calendars. Help the children draw the grid, leaving a 2-by-2-inch square for each date. Leave space above the grid for the names of days, month, season, and year.

September

Sun.	Mon.	Tues.	Wed.	Thurs.	Fri.	Sat.
						PICNIC 5
		1	2	3	4	
6	LABOR DAY 7	SCHOOL! 8	9	10	11	SWIM 12
13	14	15	16	17	18	ball game 19
dinner Grandmas 20	21	22	23	24	SPELL- ING TEST 25	26
27	28	29	MARION'S BIRTH- DAY 30			

4. Write the month, season, and year on top of the grid. Fill in the day-names.

5. Explain that, though all weeks begin on Sunday, months may begin on any day.

6. Start the children out with day number 1, then let them number the days from there.

7. Look ahead to special days. Draw a picture to symbolize parties, picnics, and so forth.

8. Each day, read out the day, date, season, and year. Do something to indicate that yesterday is past (you can draw a line through the square) and to focus on today. You may count the days between today and a special day, but be sure to emphasize that *every day* is special.

What Else

When a major exciting event such as Christmas is coming, let the children make a paper chain out of strips of construction paper or old magazine or greeting card pictures. Make one "link" for each day between now and the event, then tear off a link at the end of each day.

Children can also make their own personal "time lines" to visually reinforce their understanding of time in their own history. Start with a length of white shelf paper or butcher paper for each child. Section the paper off into blocks equal to each child's age. Have the child paste personal snapshots at each age within the appropriate blocks.

LIKE CLOCKWORK: TELLING TIME

Learning to tell time gives the child much more than useful knowledge. Telling time brings the child a new avenue of self-sufficiency in the daily routine. While waiting for a friend to arrive, a favorite television show to start, or an outing to begin, the child can consult the clock and plan his or her activity accordingly.

After some practice with organizing activities by the clock, the child will eventually gain an "inner time clock" that will tell the youngster that waiting "a few minutes" before going to the swimming pool is actually pretty easy. This inner timepiece will also tell that child that when the wait is an hour and a half, there is plenty of time to enjoy a good book before departure time.

SETTING THE STAGE
Invite the child to tell time:

> Learning to tell time means more than being able to wear your own watch. What is really great about learning this new skill is what it enables you to do on your own.

> You can organize your own time so that when your mom or dad says, "We'll be leaving for the park in fifteen minutes," you don't have to keep asking, "When are we going to go?" You can spend your waiting time doing better things like reading a book or using a building set in your room.

WHAT YOU'LL NEED
1. 1 9-inch plain white paper plate
2. Felt pen
3. 1 strip of colored paper, 5½ by ¾ inch
4. Scissors

5. Ruler
6. 1 brad
7. Hourglass type of egg timer

HOW TO DO IT

1. Write numbers on the plate so that it resembles a clock.
2. Cut the paper so you have 2 arrows, one 3½ inches long and the other 2 inches long.
3. Superimpose the strips so the nonpointed ends are slightly overlapped. Stick the brad through this end, and then place the brad in the exact center of the plate. Set this visual aid aside.
4. Turn the hourglass over and invite the children to watch the sand empty into the bottom section. Then say, "Time has passed." Do this again.
5. Tell the children that each time you turned over the hourglass you measured the time that was passing. Tell them that even now, when the sand is *not* moving in the hourglass, time is still passing. Say that today people have watches or clocks with numbers on them for measuring time.
6. Take out the clock that you made and ask the youngsters to identify all the numbers.
7. Move the long hand so that it is pointing to the number 12 and say, "Now when we tell time, we are going to keep the long hand pointing to the 12."
8. Tell the children that the short hand indicates the hour. Move the short hand to number 1 and say, "This says one o'clock." Continue this procedure to identify several other times on the clock.
9. Say, "We're going to leave the long hand pointing to the 12. The short hand indicates the hour." Then ask each child to show you, by manipulating the clock's hands, several different times.
10. Change the clock so that it reads different times. Give each child several turns to "tell the time" for you.

What Else

To teach "half-past the hour," move the small hand halfway between numbers on the clock, and move the long hand from the 12 to the 6. Explain what you've done as follows: "I am moving the small hand halfway between 1 and 2. I am moving the long hand halfway around the clock. The time is half-past one." Invite the children to participate as you did in steps 8 through 10.

To give the child who can count to 59 mastery of telling time, point out the small markings on the clock that indicate minutes. Tell the child that the small hand indicates the hour (if the hand is between two numbers, you read the smallest one), and that to measure the amount of time past the hour you only need to count the "minute markings," starting at the very top of the clock. The child will eventually come to recognize the five-minute segments on the clock as five-, ten-, and fifteen-minute intervals. But to insure the child's complete understanding of this time concept, be sure to start with a large clock that has individual minutes marked on it.

MEASURING UP (THE METRIC WAY)

Adults have been gradually preparing themselves for the great conversion from the English to metric standards of measurement. This has caused no small wave of anxiety and confusion in the hearts and minds of anyone over the age of eighteen. However, young children with their freshness of mind and enthusiastic spirit of learning can easily make this transition.

The key to success is in setting up a metric environment in which the child will learn not about converting from one system to another, but simply how to use one standard of measurement. The following activity will give the children (and *you*) practice in experiencing the elusive *ml*, not in its relation to teaspoons, tablespoons, or cups but as a specific quantity. (You may even discover that the metric system is actually easier!)

SETTING THE STAGE
Invite the child to take some measurements:

What if you invited your best friend over for lunch and you wanted to make something really special? You know that your friend loves chocolate chip cookies—who doesn't—so you decide that they will be the special treat at your luncheon.

You check around the kitchen to make sure you have all the ingredients. You do. You're all set to go until you read the recipe and see the amounts needed of each ingredient. Instead of the usual *c* for cup or *tsp* for teaspoon, you see the letters *ml* after each ingredient. You don't know what it means, but you're suddenly convinced that you'll never have enough ingredients, because the first thing you see is *125 ml butter!*

That seems like an awful lot, but actually it's the same amount you would normally use to make chocolate chip cookies. It is just a different method of measuring.

Ml stands for *milliliters.* Countries other than the United States use this system, called the International System of Units. You may hear it referred to as the *metric system.* Pretty soon, even people in the United States will use metrics.

You can get a head start in learning all about metrics and make a tasty batch of cookies in the process by following this recipe.

WHAT YOU'LL NEED

1. 125 ml butter or margarine
2. 50 ml granulated sugar
3. 100 ml brown sugar, firmly packed
4. 1 egg, well beaten
5. 5 ml vanilla
6. 450 ml all-purpose flour
7. 2.5 ml baking soda
8. 2.5 ml salt
9. 150 ml chocolate chips
10. 100 ml chopped nuts or raisins
11. Metric measuring cup and spoons (usually available at department stores)
12. Mixing bowl
13. 2 cookie sheets
14. Mixing spoon
15. Sifter
16. Metric ruler

HOW TO DO IT

1. Cream the butter and sugar together.
2. Add the well-beaten egg and the vanilla. Mix well.
3. Sift together the flour, baking soda, and salt. Gradually add the mixture to the above.
4. Stir in the chocolate chips and nuts or raisins.
5. Drop small spoonfuls of the mixture onto a greased cookie sheet, about 5 cm apart.
6. Bake in a 180 degree centigrade (350 degree Fahrenheit) oven for about 8 minutes.

What Else

Think metric! Whenever you have measuring to do, make a quick conversion to the metric equivalent. *Do this only once!* You'll come to know that "this much" flour is 200 ml through *using* this standard of measurement, rather than converting, as you smoothly teach the child straight metric measure. To gain extra practice, set up a measuring exercise in which the child can measure flour, beans, or rice from a bowl to a measuring cup and back again.

Children can also benefit—and so will you—from taking air and body temperatures using degrees centigrade. (A certain temperature comes to mind if you hear it is "78°F" outside. Soon you'll instinctively know what it's like if it's "14°C" outside.)

Finally, invite the children to make a metric map by taking the dimensions of a room and its contents using a metric ruler.

For a free booklet, "Metric Information for Kids," send a postcard to: National Bureau of Standards, Administration Building A600, Washington, DC 20234.

A SHAPE IS A CLOSED CURVE:
EXPLORING POSSIBILITIES WITH SHAPES

Most of us learned to visually recognize shapes at age five. All was well till sophomore geometry. When those familiar old triangles became objects of none-too-pleasant mystery and intrigue. What was once a friendly three-sided object suddenly became a mass of B's, H's, and ½'s!

How much easier it would have been if, when we learned to recognize these shapes, we also had had a chance to explore their parameters. Then, some ten years later, when we were faced with proofs and theorems, we would have welcomed them as additional information about old and good friends.

The following activity teaches children to recognize shapes, to learn correct terminology, and to discover the relationships of the parts to the whole, in a creative, multisensory, not to mention Montessori-inspired, fashion. It awakens an awareness of external surfaces and forms, and it gives children a real head start in the academic game. A quatrefoil may be totally unheard of to most of us adults; to the child who approaches geometry in the following manner, however, it is no more unusual than the triangle. What's more, it's prettier!

SETTING THE STAGE

Invite the children to discover what a shape actually is:

Imagine that you had a long piece of string. Pretend you are holding one end of the string with one hand and the other end with your other hand. Pull your hands as far apart as they can possibly go without breaking or dropping the imaginary string.

Do you know what the string has become? A straight line.

Now, bring your hands together so that the two ends of the string meet. Put the string on a table. What do you have now?

A *shape*. A shape is any figure that is made from a single line whose ends are joined together. But because it is made from a single line that does not cross over itself, we call it a *curve*. And because both ends of that curve come together, we call it a *closed* curve.

I'll bet two of your favorite closed curves are hearts and stars. Would you like to meet some others?

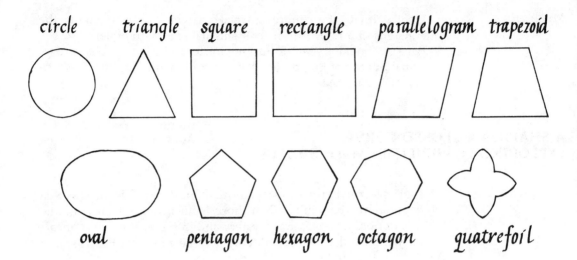

circle   triangle   square   rectangle   parallelogram   trapezoid

oval   pentagon   hexagon   octagon   quatrefoil

WHAT YOU'LL NEED

1. Posterboard or matboard
2. Mat knife
3. Pencil
4. Ruler
5. Compass
6. Felt pen
7. Paper
8. Colored pencils
9. Stapler

HOW TO DO IT

1. Cut the posterboard into twelve 6-inch squares.
2. Make a shape template (or stencil) out of each square by first drawing the shape on the square (as large as possible without cutting through the outside edge of the square), and then cutting it out. Make one for each of the following shapes:

circle	hexagon
triangle	pentagon
square	octagon
rectangle	oval
parallelogram	ellipse
trapezoid	quatrefoil

3. Write the name of each shape in block letters underneath it.
4. Turn the children loose with the templates, lots of 6-by-six-inch paper, colored pencils, and a sturdy worktable. Show them how to trace the shapes by putting the paper under the template, then tracing along the cut-out portion of the square. Encourage the

children to start each new shape by saying—or even copying—its name and tracing it, first with their fingers, then with a continuous pencil line.

5. Have each child make a "Shape Book" consisting of twelve pages on which each of the shapes have been clearly traced and labeled.

What Else

Once the children have explored all of the shapes and are familiar with each of them, the creativity begins. The youngsters can use the templates as vehicles for color mixing. The triangle can be filled in first with red pencil, for example, then topped with blue to make one purple triangle.

The boys and girls can combine different shapes to make fancy designs. They can overlap the same shape several times on a larger piece of paper. They can alternate coloring or shading techniques within single templates or fill each shape with lots of little shapes. In short, they can create anything and everything with the templates. The more these lucky girls and boys manipulate these shapes, the greater will be their understanding and enjoyment of them.

Another tactile way to explore shapes is to stretch rubber bands about the points of a geoboard, which is easily made by penciling off a grid of 1" squares on a board, then hammering nails into each intersection. And to give the children an opportunity to put their new-found acquaintance with shapes to imaginative use, accompany them on a "shape hunt" in your own neighborhood.

For an added bonus to the children's experimentation with shapes, have a story hour with *A Kiss Is Round* by Budney and *Square Is a Shape* by Sharon Lerner. You might also want to explore the shapes that can be made by folding paper, which may well lead your group to a fascinating study of the beautiful Oriental art of origami.

SEASON WATCHING

Changing seasons connote different things to different people. Many adults greet each season with the predictable exclamation, "Is it that time already?" For most children, a change of seasons is synonymous with the change in the type of clothing they wear as well as where and how long they may play.

Experiencing the seasons is inevitable, and learning from them is a real treat. By establishing and maintaining a neighborhood "season lookout point," the children will observe the order in nature and the purpose of each stage in the progression of seasons.

SETTING THE STAGE

Invite the child to do some seasonal investigation.

How can you tell what season it is?

The weather? Where you can go to play?

What if you lived your whole life inside a house with one window that overlooked a garden with flowers and a huge maple tree. Would you still be able to identify the seasons?

How?

WHAT TO DO BEFORE YOU GO

1. Make a sign stating. "This place is the official neighborhood season-watching station."
2. Discuss what spot in your neighborhood changes the most within each season (flora, play equipment left outside, house decorations).
3. Once you decide on a place, make a list of the things in the area that you and the children will observe (tree branches, moisture, clothing of children walking past).
4. Gather up the sign, a small tack or nail, paper, and pencils, and be on your way.

WHAT TO DO WHILE YOU'RE THERE

1. Post the sign.
2. Have the children write short descriptions of the area or draw pictures of it.
3. Be sure the children note what it is about the area that lets you know what season it is now.
4. Take turns making predictions as to what the area will look like when you return for your next observation.

WHAT TO DO AFTERWARD

1. Mark the date of your next observation on your calendar.
2. On 4 large sheets of paper, list all the things associated with each season. Be sure all the children contribute.

3. Make collages using pictures of clothing, recreational activities, and the natural environment during each season.
4. Make a collective collage using natural objects indicative of the season.
5. Photograph the children in front of your season-watching station. This is a great way to document the change of seasons and the changes taking place in the growing children. Try to find a tall post you can drive into the ground (or an obliging tree trunk) upon which you can log the children's heights throughout the year.
6. Stage a reenactment of the path the Earth takes around the sun in the course of a year. Have a child hold a globe (or even a ball or balloon with the continents marked on it) at the correct angle (23½°). Mark off the Earth's orbit on the floor with chalk or masking tape and have another child stand in the middle of the orbit holding a bright light. As the Earth moves around the sun, note how the light is more or less intense depending on the position of the Earth. Explain that when one part of the Earth faces the sun, it receives a more intense concentration of sunlight, which makes that place warmer. As the Earth continues to revolve around the sun, that same hemisphere is tilted away from the sun, which means the same amount of sunlight is spread over a larger area. The sunlight is not as intense, and therefore, the weather is colder.
7. Read *The Wonderful Tree,* by Adelaide Holl.

BOOKS FOR CONTINUING DISCOVERY

Books for Adults

BURNS, MARILYN. *I Hate Mathematics Book.* Boston: Little, Brown, 1978.

HALLAMORE, ELIZABETH. *The Metric Book.* Woodbury, N.Y.: Barron's Educational Series, 1974.

Books for Children

BUDNEY, BLOSSOM, *A Kiss Is Round,* New York: Lothrop, Lee, and Shepard Co., 1954.

EMBERLEY, ED. *Wing on a Flea: A Book about Shapes.* Boston: Little, Brown, 1961.

HOLL, ADELAIDE. *The Wonderful Tree.* New York: Golden Press, 1974.

KEATS, EZRA JACK. *Over in the Meadow.* New York: Scholastic Book Service, 1971.

Mathematics

LERNER, SHARON. *Square Is a Shape.* Minneapolis, Minn.: Lerner Publishing, 1970.

REISS, JOHN J. *Numbers.* New York: Bradbury Press, 1971.

SCARRY, RICHARD. *Richard Scarry's Great Big School House.* New York: Random House, 1969.

WILDSMITH, BRIAN. *Brian Wildsmith's 1,2,3.* New York: Franklin Watts, Inc., 1965.

WILDSMITH, BRIAN. *Brian Wildsmith's Puzzles.* New York: Franklin Watts, Inc., 1970.

WILDSMITH, BRIAN. *Seasons.* New York: Oxford University Press, 1980.

CHAPTER SIX

READING, WRITING, AND BOOKS

AN APPLE FROM THE TEACHER

Who would ever guess that an infant's playful cooing and a quick round of pat-a-cake would form the cornerstone of purposeful thinking and effective communication? Every time a child focuses on the spoken word and eventually tries to imitate it, he or she has begun to dabble with the infinite possibilities of language.

The child gradually understands that specific expressions elicit specific responses, and language skills begin to free the child. No longer is the youngster's life left to chance. The more clearly the child can think and express inner thoughts, the more control he or she will have over the course his or her life is to take.

Once the child is at home with language, the desire to expand his or her understanding and use of it is as lively as was the initial desire to speak. And that's precisely where "Reading, Writing, and Books" comes in. Activities in this chapter encourage the initial phases of language development and offer a variety of ways to keep this growth alive by focusing on the child's relationship with both verbal and written communication. By keeping in mind a few simple techniques, this relationship will steadily grow.

First, call a spade a spade. Speak to children clearly and intelligently. A hydrangea becomes special when it is given its proper name and is not just an anonymous botanical wonder nestled in the backyard.

Answer questions simply and precisely. If you don't know the answer, say so. Entertain some possible answers with the child or toss in a question or two of your own, such as, "What do you think happened?" "What else could have caused that?" By the same token, make statements with questions. For example, "What causes the cracks in the sidewalk? Do you think the people who live here did that? Or did the earth beneath the cement move on its own?" (In exchanges of this type, offer the desired response last so that it is easier for the child to recall.)

When the focus shifts from spoken to written languages, some new rules apply: Whenever practical, sound out words together or just identify beginning or ending sounds of words. These words can be on street signs, on cereal boxes, or in books and magazines. If you find yourself someplace where you have nothing to do but wait, play a game such as "I spy with my little eye something that begins with 'y.' " Then proceed to find all the things around you that begin with that sound.

Reading is not just for books. Reading skills begin with carefully noting the similarities and differences in the environment, then reading sounds, then reading lists or booklets of short, phonetic words. "Training Your Eyes and Ears to Read," "What Does the 'A' Say?" and "Secret Books" are activities in this chapter that provide just such a progression of basic skills.

Once the child does read words or books, you needn't feel obligated to hear every word that is read. Give the child a certain amount of time with you, and then explain that he or she can read five more pages or ten more words independently. This will work to both your advantages.

Finally, always have a variety of writing materials available for your child to use so that when the urge comes on to write a letter, word, or sentence, the youngster won't be hampered by a lack of tools. To that end, recycle any scrap paper that is blank on one side.

Language skills are essential to the child's life. When the growth and development of these skills are fully attended to, the child will come to know the joy of gaining new knowledge and acting on it in a purposeful way. Through the mastery of language skills, the child becomes an important member of the community. He or she goes out to others with the confidence of one who not only has something special to offer but also has the skill to effectively express those thoughts and feelings in a meaningful way.

TRAINING YOUR EYES AND EARS TO READ

Many people are surprised to learn that three- and four-year-old children can learn to read. But what is even more amazing is that children actually prepare to learn to read from birth, and they do so in ways that have nothing to do with letters or storybooks.

Before children can recognize and work with the subtle differences in the shapes and sounds of letters, they need to refine the tools that will enable them to do so. That is to say, young eyes and ears need to become finely tuned so they will be able to work just a little harder to get ready to read.

SETTING THE STAGE

Invite the children to exercise eyes and ears in a special way:

Sometimes things aren't always what they seem. You can easily tell the difference between a watermelon and a grape. But can you tell the difference between a tangelo and an orange?

And think of all the times you have been confused by things you hear or even see. Was the telephone ringing in your house or was that just the TV? Are the flowers in your living room real or artificial?

No matter what you're doing, you should always be training your eyes and ears to work better. This will allow them to help you to know exactly what it is you're looking at or listening to. And what could be more important when you are reading!

WHAT YOU'LL NEED
1. Several objects that make noise, such as a rattle, a bell, 2 sticks, a whistle, and a tambourine.

HOW TO DO IT (PRESENTATION I)
1. Show the children each "instrument" and demonstrate the sound it makes.
2. Ask the children to close their eyes.
3. Play each instrument. Remember the sequence.
4. Invite the children to take turns playing the instruments in the same sequence.

HOW TO DO IT (PRESENTATION II)

1. Arrange the instruments in a row in front of the children. Have the children look carefully at the arrangement.
2. Ask the children to close their eyes.
3. Rearrange the instruments in a row.
4. Ask a child to rearrange the instruments back to their original position.
5. Continue this "rearrangement" game until all the children have had a turn.

What Else

There are many ways you can continue to help train children's eyes and ears to read through spontaneous play. Imitate hand-clapping patterns during a rest time or whenever you and the children are in need of some quick, but not too strenuous, entertainment, such as when you are filling time in a waiting room. Or you can take turns imitating a series of body movements.

For a different kind of entertainment when friends get together, have a child sit blindfolded in a chair and have another child stand behind the chair and sing a song. The blindfolded child must guess the identity of the singer.

To make a matching game, simply gather pairs of pretty household objects or pictures, mix them up, and have the children match the pairs. Or set up patterns with colored blocks, pegs, beads or building blocks and have the children duplicate them.

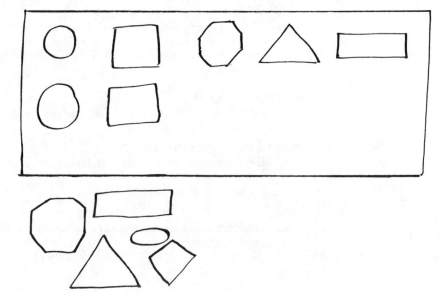

Finally, make a picture lotto game. Start with two sets of pictures. Glue one set on a piece of railroad board and glue the other pictures on individual pieces of railroad board. Have the child match the pictures on the individual cards to the pictures on the large card.

WHAT DOES THE "A" SAY?

Thanks to creative children's television programming, many toddlers can easily recognize and recite the alphabet. This is a great auditory and visual exercise for these children but, sadly, it has practically nothing to do with reading. Knowing that *a* and *t* are spoken as *ay* and *tee* will not help the child decode *at*.

Children who long to read can easily learn the name of the letter as well as the sound it makes. While not all words are phonetic, a great many are. This allows the avid young reader to easily build a large reading vocabulary with relative independence once he or she learns what the *a* and all the rest say.

SETTING THE STAGE
Invite the child to take the first step in learning to read:

Think of your favorite storybook, and about how much fun it is to sit with someone you like a lot and have that person read to you.

But what if you wanted to hear the story and no one was around to read it to you? Or suppose you wanted to read your special story to a special friend? Well, it takes a lot of skill to be able to read a whole book, but you can start out by learning to read sounds. Sounds make words. And words are what make a whole book!

WHAT YOU'LL NEED
1. 26 blank 3-by-5-inch cards
2. Blue and red large-tipped felt pens

HOW TO DO IT
1. Write one lower-case letter on each card, with vowels in one color and consonants in another.
2. Present the letters to the children in pairs, using the following three-step procedure. (Always remember to introduce the letter by its *sound* rather than its name). Trace the letter with your index and middle finger. Say "This is *a*." (Use the short vowel pronunciation.) Have the child trace the letter and say the sound. Then remove the letter and get out another one (for example, *t*) and follow the same procedure.
   • Place both letters (the *a* and the *t)* in front of the child and say, "Show me *a*," then, "Show me *t*."

• Place one of the letters in front of the child and ask, "What is this?"
3. If the child gives a wrong answer at any stage, simply go back to the previous question. There is no need to bring attention to the mistake as such.
4. Continue the three-step procedure for the entire alphabet.

What Else

Play games to name words that begin with certain sounds. Look around the room or name objects in a certain category in alphabetical order. For example, if the category is "Things you find at the beach," you might say "A—abalone, B—bathing suit, C—clam."

Children might also enjoy cutting pictures out of a magazine and making a collage of things beginning with the same sound.

Finally, read one of the many alphabet books that are available. P. D. Eastman's *The Alphabet Book* gives a whimsical twist to phonetics.

DOT-TO-DOT WORDS

An interesting aspect of language development is that children can learn to read before they can learn to write. But what better way is there to reinforce a new reading vocabulary than by writing it down?

Dot-to-dot words provide a way to both reinforce reading skills and train little hands to write, so that one day the dots won't be necessary.

SETTING THE STAGE
Invite the child to practice penmanship:

Remember when it was your grandfather's birthday and your parents wanted you to sign the card? Or that time you made a really neat painting at school and wanted to write your name on it so it wouldn't get lost?

You knew exactly how to spell your name, but when it came to writing it down, you needed some help.

Well, now there's something you can do about that problem so that your fingers will soon be able to do just what your mind wants them to.

WHAT YOU'LL NEED
1. Pens and pencils
2. Several sheets of 8½-by-11-inch paper

HOW TO DO IT
1. With a pen, print the child's name several times on a sheet of paper. Instead of using solid lines, use a series of dots or dashes to form the shape of each letter.

Douglas

cake

letter

visit

library

farm

museum

2. Mark the dot on each letter where the child should first place the pencil with an arrow or the number 1. If the child needs to pick up the pencil before completing each letter, write a number 2 where the pencil should be placed to finish forming the letter.
3. Have the child trace each letter according to the numerical instructions beginning on the left side of each.

What Else

Now that the child is comfortable with the exercise, have several Xerox copies made of dot-to-dot words so that there will always be plenty on hand. Be sure to emphasize that even though there are lots of sheets, there is no need to rush.

You can increase the child's sight vocabulary by sitting with the youngster and thinking of other dot-to-dot word lists. They can be friends' names, favorite foods, planets, or maybe new silly-sounding words. (*Rutabaga,* for example, *sounds* a lot funnier than it really is!)

Or if tracing words is a little overwhelming for the child, make tracing sheets of individual letters, or even several repetitions of shapes that are found in letters (for example, straight lines, circles, or semicircles formed in different directions).

For the child who needs to refine the ability to control a pencil, make railroad board templates in geometric shapes. Put the template on a blank piece of paper and have the child trace inside the shape with a pencil. Then have the youngster carefully draw several straight lines or other small designs within the shape.

SECRET BOOKS: WORDS TO SOUND OUT

One of the greatest benefits to teaching reading phonetically is that with this basic knowledge, the children can easily expand their reading vocabularies on their own. Many primary storybooks are composed mostly of phonetic words; once children know the basic phonetic sounds of the alphabet, they can independently read through these books or even pick out phonetic words in a more difficult book or magazine.

By writing out words in their own books, children reinforce their ability to read a word smoothly (rather than sounding out a word as nothing more than a choppy series of single sounds) because they are more actively involved with it. When these words are written out and bound in a "secret book," they take on a special quality. "These are *my* words," says the child, and it is a privilege for the youngster to share them. What's more, the secret book will give the child a new sense of pride: It is a whole book that he or she can read unaided.

SETTING THE STAGE

Invite the children to make their very own books that they can read all by themselves:

Who can think of a word that rhymes with *cat? Fat? Sat?* You have just named many words in one "family." This family is called the *at* family.

Now that you know this family, you can keep it with you always and share it with whomever you wish. Do you know how?

By making a secret book!

WHAT YOU'LL NEED
1. Pens or pencils
2. Several pieces of paper, about 2 by 4 inches
3. Several pieces of construction paper, about 3 by 5 inches
4. Stapler

HOW TO DO IT
1. Have each child write the word *at* in the middle of 8 to 10 pieces of paper. (Use more as needed.)
2. On each sheet, have the child write a consonant in front of *at* so that a word is formed. (For example, *cat* is acceptable, but *dat* is not.)
3. Using the construction paper for front and back covers, staple the pages together to make a book.

What Else

The children may like to reinforce this new skill with a new medium. They can use magnetic letters on a refrigerator or metal board to make the words.

The child can easily recite the new vocabulary if it is listed on an adding machine tape that is hung at eye level.

Finally, add some literary creativity to the secret books by inviting the children to make up rhyming sentences; if a child happens to be especially clever, he or she may write a very short story composed mainly of words of the same family or group of similar families.

Other phonetic word families you can use are: *ab, ad, ag, al, am, an, ap, ed, eg, en, et, ib, id, ig, im, in, ip, it, ob, od, og, om, on, op, ot, ub, ug, um, un, up.*

"DEAR DIARY"

Small children have incredible memories of events that relate directly to themselves. Just ask any child about a long-past occasion of particular personal significance, and you'll be dazzled by the uncannily accurate recall of the slightest details.

This fantastic memory is, to a certain extent, a function of the small child's natural self-absorption. You can capitalize on this aspect of the child's nature by teaching the youngster to begin a diary.

The benefits of such an activity are many. First and foremost, the child will be learning and practicing skills related to clear thinking and clear writing. Pure "stream of consciousness" writing can evolve into clear, concise journalistic prose. On another level, keeping a diary will provide the child with many opportunities to reflect on his or her own life. At best, the diary can serve as a chronicle of self-growth. At the very least, it will record those "favorite things" and special events that somehow made an impression on the child at this point in time.

Diary making is by no means limited to children who can write. Pictorial diaries can be excellent ways for the younger children to create a lasting and beautiful record of memorable moments in their lives.

SETTING THE STAGE
Invite the children to discover the pleasures of keeping a diary:

Do you have a favorite book? Is it about someone special? How would you like to have a book about the most special person you know? *Written* by that same special person?

Can you guess who that special person might be? It's *you!*

Wouldn't it be fun to open a book such as this and read about all the exciting things that happened on your last birthday, or the fun you had on last year's summer vacation?

Such a book is called a *diary,* and today I'll show you how to keep one. It's actually quite simple: Just write down some words or draw some pictures each day that express your special thoughts to tell about special things.

WHAT YOU'LL NEED
1. A notebook for each child, preferably with stitched rather than looseleaf bindings so that the child won't be tempted to tear out pages
2. Old magazines containing pictures of children and children-oriented subjects
3. Scraps of fabric, lace, or yarn
4. Scissors
5. Glue
6. Paper
7. Marking pens and crayons
8. Pens

HOW TO DO IT
1. Let each child choose a notebook and then personalize it by decorating the jacket with cutouts, fabric, or drawings, and by printing his or her name in fancy letters on it.

2. Write today's day and date in large letters on a sheet of paper. Place it where all the children can see it. Instruct the children to write the day and date on top of the first page in the book.
3. Invite the children to think silently about today. Are they happy? Sad? Is the weather nice? Has something exciting happened? What favorite things can they think of? Is there any one thing about today they would like to remember always?
4. When the children have had time to reflect, direct them to write some of these thoughts, or illustrate them with drawings, on today's diary page.
5. Explain to the children that if they wish to keep a diary, they should do this every day.

What Else

One way to extend the diary-making activity is to invite the children to turn back to any day and date and then write a story based on what they recorded that day. Older children can use their diaries as the basis for a writing exercise: Starting with any entry, have the future journalists elaborate on and perfect their writing in a finished piece they can share with the group.

Unique diary entries can be made by utilizing *synoptic pictures,* a form of mural that pictorially represents what happened before, during, and after an event.

Finally, children may enjoy recording a whole day's events and feelings through one page of illustrations.

"WHAT IF . . .": PICTURE BOOKS
FOR ANY SITUATION

The following activity formally introduces the child to the imagination, and gives the youngster a chance to see this marvelous force at work.

"What if . . ." books are books that can be written without any writing skills whatsoever. Because the thoughts are communicated through pictures, with just the slightest creative nudge from an interested adult, a child who has yet to learn to read can still be the author of an exciting and imaginative tale.

Through this activity, children can become acquainted with aspects of the problem-solving process. They can explore alternative outcomes and their consequences as they "write" their stories. This is not only a valuable exercise in creativity; it also helps the children to deal with similar situations that occur in daily life.

Finally, the following activity facilitates verbal communication in the child. The child must think clearly at the "telling" stage to get the story across. This clarity of thought and expression, in turn, lays the foundation for more advanced writing.

SETTING THE STAGE

Invite the child to envision a "what if . . ." situation:

What if all your friends came over? And you planned to go on a picnic? And what if it rained?

What could you do instead?

Thinking about "what if's" is called *imagining.* Your imagination lets you picture things in your mind that may never have happened, things you may have dreamed about, or even things you thought were never possible.

Though imagining is something you do in your mind, you can also do it on paper.

WHAT YOU'LL NEED

1. Plain white paper, 8½ by 11 inches
2. Stapler
3. Scissors
4. Pencils
5. Crayons

HOW TO DO IT

1. Fold each sheet of paper into fourths. Staple one side and cut open the folded sides.
2. Help the children to imagine "what if" situations. Here are a few examples: "What if I went to visit grandma and she had just finished building a bookcase and she had some wood left over?" or "What if I got invited to a birthday party on the moon?"
3. Have each child draw a picture on each page of the book that tells something about what might happen during that situation. The children may color the pictures.
4. Invite the children to take turns telling a story to the group based upon the pictures in their books.

What Else

Children may well have a different story to tell each time they "read" their books. This is an excellent way for them to exercise their creative juices; it also helps foster a genuine respect and love for books.

If any of the books are especially exciting or humorous, turn them into plays or puppet shows. Let the author become the director.

You might discuss other uses of the imagination, too. For example, artists use their imaginations to help them paint pictures. Both adults and children use their imaginations to solve problems and have fun.

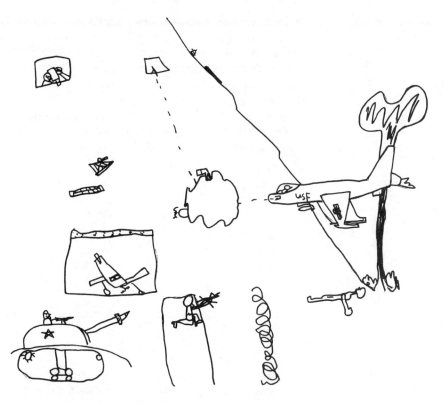

And sometimes imaginations do another job for children: They create imaginary friends. This may be a good time to share tales about imaginary playmates. You might even tell the children about one you had as a child. This little discussion can be an excellent way to remind the child that these friends exist only in the imagination while offering reassurance that pals of the imaginary variety are still OK to have!

HOW COLESLAW GOT ITS NAME

As adults, we occasionally find ourselves baffled by the origins of some of the words that creep into our conversation. What does *taxidermy*, for example, have to do with *taxicabs*? Or since when it is the common ordinary "bad guy" a *mountebank*? Imagine, then, how silly everyday words like *coleslaw* or *caterpillar* can seem to the young child to whom a good portion of the language is unfamiliar to start with!

"How Coleslaw Got Its Name" is an activity that delves into the origins of words with a sense of fun and adventure. Children who participate in this exercise will gain some insight into the development of language as they learn to appreciate the contributions of other cultures. They will also begin to see the logic behind illogical-sounding words. As the youngsters become more familiar with the sources of words, they will start recognizing roots and may well be able to figure out definitions of some new words on their own. Ideally, once this happens, they will use words with confidence; they will be increasingly intrigued by new words and will expand their vocabularies daily.

This activity also gives children practice using a dictionary, and exposes them to the wealth of information contained there.

SETTING THE STAGE

Invite the girls and boys to consider the origin of a silly-sounding word:

How do *you* think coleslaw got its name?

It isn't made of coal. And it surely isn't a "slaw," whatever that might be. So why did someone name it *coleslaw?*

Coleslaw is a word we borrowed from the Dutch. It comes from the Dutch word for cabbage, which is *kool,* and the Dutch word for salad, which is *salade.*

The Dutch put *kool* and *salade* together, and came up with *koosla.* In America, we say *coleslaw.*

There are many different languages in the world. The language people speak in America is called *English.* Many English words are borrowed from words from other languages. And some words come from English words or names from long, long ago. That's why many of our words, like *coleslaw,* sound like something other than what they really are.

Finding out how something got its name is called finding the word's *etymology.* You can do this just by looking in the dictionary.

WHAT YOU'LL NEED
1. Paper
2. Pens or pencils
3. Dictionary

HOW TO DO IT
1. Have the children write these words on a piece of paper: *caterpillar, dandelion, kindergarten, sandwich, tadpole.* Leave space under each word.
2. Have each child draw a picture of what each word is, then draw a picture or pictures of what each word *sounds* like it is. This can be done by breaking the word into recognizable parts (For example, "sand" and "witch") or by picturing the entire concept (a "dandy lion"). The child may also want to make a whimsical illustration of the image the word creates.
3. Pass around each child's pictures. Talk about them, and take turns guessing how each of these things may have gotten its name.

4. Turn to the etymology key in the front of the dictionary. Show it to the children and demonstrate how to look up etymologies in the dictionary.

5. One by one, look up each word in the dictionary and explain its etymology, or origin, to the children. Talk about how the word-name follows from its sources.

6. If the children's interest continues, have them pursue the activity with other words they may have wondered about.

What Else

Of course, we haven't borrowed all our words from other languages. Many of our words are English to start with, and many of them—like compound words—are "borrowed" from our own language.

Some compound words the children are familiar with are *bathroom, seaweed, horseshoe, undershirt,* and *lunchbox.* See if they can think of any others.

You may want to explain to the children that we use compound words because it simplifies our language. It is easier to say "overcoat," for example, than it is to say "coat that you wear over your other clothes." In this light, have the children try to make up brand-new compound words, or compound phrases such as *breakfast room* or *coffee table.*

Finally, since the children have become somewhat familiar with the dictionary, think up some other dictionary games. For example, say an unfamiliar (but not too obscure) word. Then give the right definition and two made-up ones. Let the children guess which is the real meaning of the word, then have them take turns looking it up to see which was right.

And for a free copy of "Interesting Origins of English Words," send a postcard to: G. & C. Merriam Company, 47 Federal Street, Springfield, MA 01101.

VISITING THE PLACE
WITH ALL THE ANSWERS

Today's child can scarcely get through grade school, much less high school, without many productive trips to the library to gather books and information. The following field trip provides a positive way to introduce young children to the library, giving them a head start on learning how to use its resources properly.

Practical benefits aside, there are other less obvious reasons for familiarizing youngsters with the library at an early age. The first of these is the psychological comfort and sense of security that comes from knowing there is a "place with all the answers" nearby. For once a child—or anyone, for that matter—becomes accustomed to visiting the library, there is never a question that can't be answered, never a day with nothing to do.

Second, by learning about *all* the services offered by the public library, the child becomes exposed to more new ideas and potential hobbies. A youngster may well take advantage of new areas of interest, such as gardening or even rock collecting, simply because they are presented in an attractive, open-ended manner.

There is also great benefit derived from participating in the library's group activities. Boys and girls from many different backgrounds can easily share their common interests in anything from *Star Wars* gadgetry to *Little House* . . . books, and may eventually become friends.

Finally, the public library is a place that grows with the child. There is something special contained there for every age group. Once the first happy acquaintance is made, the child will always have a comfortable niche where he or she will be welcome to learn, to grow, and simply to enjoy.

SETTING THE STAGE

Invite the children to discover the wealth of knowledge contained within the library:

> When was the last time you asked a question? What was it about? Did you learn something new when you got your answer? Would you like to know more about the answer you received?
>
> Wouldn't it be great if there was a place where you could go to get any answer to any question you could think of?
>
> Well, there is such a place. In fact, there is probably a place like this very close to where we are right now. It is open almost every day, and there are people there who are happy to help you learn whatever it is you want to learn.
>
> This is a place where you may have gone to see a puppet show, watch a movie, listen to stories, or hear music. This is a place where you can even join a garden club.
>
> Have you guessed what kind of special place can give you so much?
>
> It's the public library!

WHAT TO DO BEFORE YOU GO

1. Telephone the library branch nearest you. Ask when it is open and what it has to offer young readers. (If this branch is not especially well equipped to serve young children, or if there is no children's librarian on hand, ask the name of another branch that is more suited to your group.)

2. Ask to speak to the children's librarian. Tell her that you plan to take a group of children to visit. Ask when would be a convenient time to do so.

3. Have each child think of something especially intriguing, such as race cars or fairy tales or blizzards or even heart transplants. Emphasize that the children can learn about *anything* at the library.

4. Gather up pencils, notebooks, and bookbags and be on your way.

WHAT TO DO WHILE YOU'RE THERE

1. Lead the children to the juvenile section and the librarian on duty there. Introduce yourselves to the librarian.

2. Let the children take turns sharing their special subjects of interest with the librarian. Invite them to ask all their questions.

3. Following the librarian's direction, help the children find the books that hold the answers to their questions.

4. Be sure the children ask the librarian the most important question of all before they leave: "What else can we do at the library?"

WHAT TO DO AFTERWARD

1. Have each child keep a notebook about trips to the library. This journal may include:
   - What the child did during this trip to the library.
   - What new things the child learned, saw, or thought about.
   - What the youngster may want to discover the next time.

2. Let the children take turns retelling (or rewriting) the ending to a story they just read.

3. Have the boys and girls design covers for their favorite book.

4. Invite the children to make some really fancy bookmarks. (These might be special gifts for the librarian who was so helpful.)

5. Make a group poster, telling other children what a great place the library is.

6. Explain to the children that storybooks are arranged alphabetically according to the author's last name, and suggest that they keep a file of books they have enjoyed, including title and author, so that the next time they go to the library, they can easily find more books by the same author that they are also likely to enjoy.

7. For lists of award-winning books children are sure to enjoy, send a stamped, self-addressed, legal-sized envelope to: Children's American Library Association, 50 East Huron St., Chicago, IL 60611. Ask for "Notable Children's Booklist," "Newberry Award Booklist," and "Caldecott Award Booklist."

8. If the children have had the opportunity of watching a puppet show at the library, they may be motivated to present one of their own. Sack, finger or sock puppets are quite easy to make. For more elaborate creations, see Peggy Davison Jenkins' *The Magic of Puppetry.*

picture on stick

finger

rag

sock

sack

THE BOOKSTORE

Many children are—happily—as familiar with the local library as they are with their city park. Books link the child with the world at large and can also catapult the child into unknown territory through his or her imagination.

Once in a while, a book will become as dear to the child as a best friend. That is the time to introduce the child to the bookstore. This will foster an interest in the child in owning books and will introduce the youngster to the wide range of possibilities in reading at every level of interest and ability.

SETTING THE STAGE
Invite the child to explore the bookstore.

> Have you ever found a book that you liked so much that you wanted to read it every day? You know you can check it out of the library any time you want, but sometimes it's not available because other people want to read it, too. Or maybe the pages are worn from so many other children reading it.
>
> Think of how special it would be to own your very own copy of this book, or others that are just as special. You'd be able to build your very own library at home!

WHAT TO DO BEFORE YOU GO
1. Discuss what you'd expect to find at a bookstore (types of books, posters, cards).
2. Make a list of reasons why you and the children think owning your own books is a good idea.
3. Phone ahead to the bookstore and let them know you will be coming. Perhaps a clerk will be available to show you around.

WHAT TO DO WHEN YOU'RE THERE

1. First, just walk around the bookstore and look at all the books.

2. Ask the clerk to tell your group a little bit about how a bookstore is run—where the books come from, how they're advertised, how the manager happens to know which books to stock.

3. Encourage each child to spend some time choosing a book he or she would like to own. The child needn't buy the book now, but may simply keep it in mind as an incentive to save money or as an idea for a birthday or Christmas present.

4. Send the children on a well-behaved treasure hunt: Have each child find a special kind of book. For example, invite the child who knows a little about animals, but who would like to know more, to find a book on zoos. Or have a very urbanized youngster look for a book on farming. Then have each child find a favorite book and a book that looks especially new and interesting to share with the group. Remind the children to be very careful with the books.

WHAT TO DO AFTERWARD
1. The children can write their own books and then have a book fair to sell them.
2. The next time the children make a book of any kind, show them how to include all the parts of a "real" book: title page, table of contents, cover, and endsheets.

BOOKS FOR CONTINUING DISCOVERY

Books for Adults

EMERY, DONALD G., PHD. *Teach Your Preschooler to Read.* New York: Simon & Schuster, 1975.

JENKINS, PEGGY DAVISON. *The Magic of Puppetry.* Englewood Cliffs, N.J.: Prentice-Hall, 1980.

LEHANE, STEPHEN. *The Creative Child.* Englewood Cliffs, N.J.: Prentice-Hall, 1979.

MARZOLLO, JEAN, and JANICE LLOYD. *Learning through Play.* New York: Harper Colophon Books, 1972.

Books for Children

EASTMON, P.D. *The Alphabet Book.* New York: Random House, 1974.

HOJA, ADRIAN. *Bear Finds a Friend.* Make-a-Book series. New York: Dell Pub. Co., Inc., 1979.

PIATTI, CELESTINO. *Celestino Piatti's Animal ABCs.* New York: Atheneum, 1966.

SENDAK, MAURICE. *Alligators All Around.* New York: Harper & Row, Pub., 1962.

WILDSMITH, BRIAN. *Brian Wildsmith's ABCs.* New York: Watts Publishing, 1963.

CHAPTER SEVEN

SCIENCE

AN APPLE FROM THE TEACHER

If you are fortunate enough to be a talented artist and you learn a new technique, your whole style of painting could be influenced. But nearly everything else in your life would stay pretty much the same. However, when you study science, you automatically enjoy many "fringe benefits" that reach far beyond the knowledge you gained about some facet of the scientific world.

Science is a systematic study of some object or phenomenon which sends scientists—young or old—into a methodical pursuit of some nugget of truth that may help make the world a more interesting and life-supporting place to be.

While knowledge gained through the scientific method is useful, the *way* in which it is gained is more useful still because the method itself serves as an exercise to develop the creative thinking process. Keen awareness of an existing situation leads the researcher to clearly identify the problem at hand and to entertain possible solutions. These, in turn, will be carefully studied through regular observations and experimentation.

This method has brought scientists many significant insights into the world and how it functions. The young scientist, when using the same scientific method, will enjoy similar success. But for these young minds, there are some extra special bonuses. While following their natural curiosity to examine something that is particularly fascinating to them, youngsters are refining their cognitive and verbal abilities. Discussing their new knowledge is also a sure way to reinforce that knowledge.

What's more, the child's spontaneous reaction to something new will naturally lead to some sort of further examination and, quite possibly, to experimentation. For instance, what young child, when given a rubber duck and a bubble bath, can resist sending that toy through the rigorous paces of bathtime play—splashing, dunking, floating? This will be so much fun that the child will naturally want to do it over and over again. Through this repetition, the child will soon observe certain patterns in the duck's behavior in the bathtub. The child will no doubt take a fancy to certain maneuvers and figure out what can be done to make them happen over and over again.

As the bathtub scientist is enjoying the rubber duck's performance, some questions may very well come to mind, such as "Why does my duck float, but my favorite rock go to the bottom?" or, "Why does my duck always pop back up when I push it to the bottom?"

Thus, the child begins to experience scientific wonder, to say, "I wonder why . . . I'll try to find out," or, "I wonder about . . . Gee! That's neat!" It is in the spirit of the latter that the former can most fully be done. And it is this sense of wonder that the young scientist will always have even if his or her particular life follows a nonscientific path. Reverence and joy in life will become synonymous with living it.

The method of inquiry born of this sense of wonder handily polishes an individual's ability to learn and understand many things, whether they are within the scientific realm or in one's personal life. This scientific line of reasoning lays the groundwork for success by leading each individual through this clear and systematic scientific thinking process: This happens. This is why. What can I do to make it happen (or prevent it from happening) again? What can I do to make what happens better?

It does not matter if the situation involves a floating duck, maintaining a special friendship, planning a party, or planting a garden; no problem will prove too great for this clear-thinking, creative person.

LEARNING ABOUT PLANTS

Everyone loves plants. They're nice to look at. They bring an attractive touch to our homes and offices. They're relatively easy to care for, and they are often the focus of many leisure hours' activity.

Plants do a lot for us, too. Their shapes and structures add infinite variety and beauty to the world. Plants also have far greater significance than their visual beauty. They give the human family food to eat and air to breathe.

Here is a chance for us to reciprocate. By teaching your children about plants in the activities to follow, you will be doing your part to assure their appreciation and cultivation for generations to come.

Seedy Things to Do in Your Own Backyard

SETTING THE STAGE

Invite the child to enjoy firsthand experience of the life cycle of a plant:

Take a look in your backyard. What makes it so pretty? Flowers and other plants are favorite additions to everyone's yards. They are easy to get and

care for, too. All you have to do is go down to your local nursery and buy some plants and bring them home.

But what if you went to the nursery and there were no plants left when you got there?

You need not feel bad, because there is another way to have a pretty garden. It takes a wee bit longer, but you'll have lots of fun in the process.

WHAT YOU'LL NEED
1. 1 package of seeds (preferably radish, squash, nasturtium, or marigold, because they sprout within a few days)
2. Trowel
3. Watering can
4. Small stick
5. Tape
6. Notebook
7. Brown and green felt pens

HOW TO DO IT
1. Have the children cultivate the soil and plant the seeds according to directions. (If your yard does not have a willing patch of soil, or if you do not have a yard, how about a nice big flowerpot for your front porch?)
2. Tape the empty package to the stick and place it in the ground where the seeds are planted.
3. Have the girls and boys use the felt pens to draw pictures of what the newly planted garden looks like. Label this "Day 1."
4. Set up a gardening schedule so that each child will be equally busy tending to the garden by doing such things as watering, weeding, and thinning the shoots each day.
5. Document the progress of the garden in pictures or short sentences in the notebook. Let the children take turns with the record keeping each day. Continue this until the garden has been harvested.

Tropisms: Smart Things for Plants to Do

SETTING THE STAGE

Invite the child to see just how smart plants really are:

If you want a glass of water, you know to go to the sink or fountain. If you're hungry, you'll go to the refrigerator. And if the room you're in is too dark, you'll lift the shade or turn on a light.

All of this is easy for you to figure out because you're an intelligent child. Plants like a lot of the same things that you like to have, and they are pretty smart about getting them, too.

WHAT YOU'LL NEED
1. 3 small clear glass jars
2. Water
3. Enough cotton to fill all the jars
4. 6 dried beans
5. 10 sheets of white paper
6. Black and green felt-tipped pens

HOW TO DO IT
1. Fill each jar with cotton that has been soaked with water.
2. Place 2 beans in each jar between the cotton and the glass. *Make sure that the scar* (the "belly button" of the bean, located in the middle of the side) *is facing in a different direction in each jar.* For example, in 1 jar, the 2 scars will face up; in the second, down; and in the last, to the side.
3. Label one paper "Day 1." On it, draw the 3 jars and exactly what the beans within look like.
4. Each day, for the next 9 days, have the children take turns recording the changes observed in all the beans.
5. On "Day 10," discuss how different parts of the seedling meet different needs: Shoots always grow up to meet the sun and roots always grow down toward the source of water. This happens with every seed that sprouts. There are no mistakes in nature!

Labeling the Parts of the Whole

SETTING THE STAGE
Invite the children to discover the plant's working parts:

If you want to walk somewhere, you use your feet. If you want to eat, you use your hands and mouth. If you want to speak, you use your voice.

There are parts of your body that let you do anything you want to do. Even though flowers may seem to be very simple things, they are just as clever as you are in many ways.

Take one apart, and discover why!

WHAT YOU'LL NEED
1. Scissors
2. Several large flowers with stems; such as tulips, fuchsias, and daffodils
3. Several 4-by-6-inch cards (6 for you and 6 for each child)
4. Tape
5. Pens

HOW TO DO IT
1. As the children watch, carefully snip the corolla, calyx, stem, pistil, and stamen of 1 flower.
2. Tape each part onto a card, and label appropriately.
3. Discuss, and write down on the card, the function of each part. Briefly, they are as follows:
   - *Corolla*—Colorful petals attract insects
   - *Calyx*—Green underside of corolla which protected it when it was still a bud
   - *Stem*—Attaches flower to main plant and conducts nutrition to the flower
   - *Pistil*—Seed producer, located in the middle of the flower
   - *Stamen*—Pollen producer, located around the pistil
   - *Ovary*—Bulb-like structure, located between the top of the stem and the corolla. It contains the seeds.
4. With the cards you just made set out as models, invite the children to dissect their own flowers and make a set of cards to keep.
5. To really liven up your dissection, sing the following song (to the tune of "I'm Looking over a Four-Leaf Clover"):

I'm looking over the parts of a flower
That I overlooked before.
First is the corolla. Second is stem.
Stamen and pistil—the bees go to them.
Then there's the ovary and the calyx
That used to be the bud.
I'm looking over the parts of a flower
That I overlooked before.

What Else

Now it's time to use all this knowledge! Have each child choose a favorite plant at a nursery or choose one that is already in the envi-

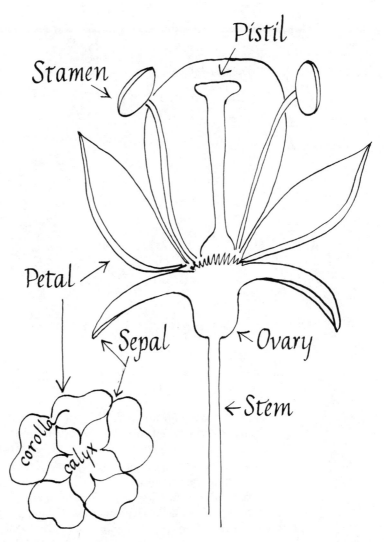

Pistil

Stamen

Petal

Sepal

Ovary

Stem

corolla

calyx

ronment to care for. This plant will be the sole responsibility of that child.

Another fun activity would be to gather a variety of seeds (one or two of each) and sprout them in a clear container. (Use the method described in "Tropisms: Smart Things for Plants to Do.") Observe the similarities and differences in the sprouting seeds. While all seeds have the same need for light, air, and water, their sprouts look different and they grow at different rates.

Children can also start new plants from old ones by rooting a leaf or stem shoot in some water. (African violet leaves, Creeping Charlie cuttings, or short vines of ivy are especially good for this.) They can also start new flowers from old. Take a faded marigold bloom, for

example, and separate and dry out the petals. Have the children compare them after a few days to store-bought marigold seeds, if you have any on hand, then plant them. After this last exercise, ask the children if they can figure out how pretty flowers that die in the winter keep coming back year after year.

Finally, share *The Remarkable Plant in Apartment 4A* by Giulio Maestro with the children as a whimsical way to wrap up this section. And to give city-dwelling children a chance to appreciate the beauty of plants, how about a visit to the florist?

LEARNING ABOUT WEATHER

"Everybody talks about the weather, but nobody does anything about it." While harnessing the clouds and shifting the wind may not be within our immediate power, there is plenty we *can* do about the *effects* weather has on our lives. We can learn to predict changes in the weather and plan what to wear and what to do accordingly.

The following activities invite the children to discover what causes different kinds of weather and what they can do about it to make themselves more comfortable. With this extra knowledge of the hows and whys of weather, our children can easily enjoy each day regardless of the temperature or humidity. Meanwhile, they can have lots of fun performing experiments and coming to some interesting conclusions about the weather.

How to Be Hot When It's Cold and Cool When It's Hot

SETTING THE STAGE

Invite the child to make some useful adjustments to the weather:

> When it's really cold, we think of how great it would be to be really hot. And when it's really hot, we think of how great it is to be really cold.

> Of course, neither extreme is that comfortable. What is best is to do a few tricks to cool down when it's hot and warm up when it's cold.

> How many of these "tricks" can you think of? Would you like to learn some new ones?

WHAT YOU'LL NEED

1. 1 piece each of dark clothing and light-colored clothing for each child, made of the same fabric
2. Jumprope
3. Water
4. Drawing paper

HOW TO DO IT

1. Have the children leave both pieces of their clothing outside in the sun for half a day. At about 2:00 P.M., have the children feel the clothes. Which are warmer? Which are cooler? Which articles would the children like to wear on chilly days? On hot days? Explain to the children that dark colors absorb light and keep what's inside nice and warm, and light colors reflect light, which is just fine on a hot summer day.

2. Have the children put on their sweaters or jackets and go outside to jump rope. After 5 minutes of jumping, ask them if they'd like to take off their "outer wear." Explain that when children play hard, their bodies burn lots of *calories* to give them energy. This creates a kind of internal furnace which warms the body from the inside out. So on a cold day, if you need to warm up, simply jump up and down!

3. Have each child wet one arm thoroughly and leave the other completely dry, then go outside to sit in the hot sun. Ask them which arm feels best. Explain that *evaporation* (the process that changes water from a liquid you can splash into a vapor you can

barely see) is what helps keep one arm cool. The more evaporation there is, the cooler the body will be.

4. Hot air gets even hotter when it is close to a warm body. Have the children fold pieces of paper into accordion pleats and fan themselves with it. Ask them how they feel when they move the hot air that is close to their body away from themselves, and move the not-so-hot air from farther away close to them.

Is the Weather Vane, Can Comas Race, and Other Measures of the Beaufort Scale

SETTING THE STAGE
Invite the children to learn about the wind as they play with it:

Because of the way the earth turns in space, and because air is always changing its temperature, we have wind.

It is interesting to study about wind, but when you're outside playing, it's lots of fun to measure the wind and play with it, too.

WHAT YOU'LL NEED
1. Black or blue pen
2. White tagboard
3. Clock
4. Soap bubbles and bubble blower
5. Kite
6. Ping-pong balls
7. Comas (dandelion puffs)

HOW TO DO IT
1. Make a 12- by 8-inch grid on the tagboard, using 1-inch squares.
2. Across the edge of the longer side, write in the times from 8:00 A.M. to 6:00 P.M. in the boxes.
3. Label the squares along the shorter side "Day 1" . . . "Day 7."
4. Using the Beaufort Scale have the children take turns writing down the wind speed for each time of each day. Take note of any patterns of wind changes each day and discuss them.
5. Now that the children know a little bit more about the wind, they can have some fun with it by blowing soap bubbles into the wind or, if the wind will cooperate, flying a kite.
6. The children can make some wind of their own inside and play this game: Have two children lay on the floor and blow ping-pong balls across the room. The child whose ball reaches the far wall first is the winner.
7. If the children can find any comas outside, they can have a similar race with them, or have contests to see who can keep their coma in the air the longest.

Beaufort Scale	
Wind Speed [miles / hour]	What Happens
1-3	chimney smoke drifts
4-7	leaves move slightly
8-12	leaves move along ground
13-18	leaves lift into air
19-24	small trees bend ~ flags fly straight
25-31	flags flap ~ umbrellas blow
32-38	small trees bend down - hard to walk against wind
39-46	tree twigs snap off
47-73	big trees blow down - buildings damaged
over 74	Hurricane!

Nimbostratus Means a Rainy Day

Invite the children to discover some clues about predicting weather:

Draw a picture of a cloud in your mind. Or think of what the last cloud you drew on paper looks like. Probably big and puffy, right?

Clouds sometimes do look like that. But sometimes they are so thin and small you can barely find them in the sky. It all depends on how high they are in the sky. And this is what tells us what the weather is going to be.

WHAT YOU'LL NEED

1. 4 sheets of blue construction paper for each child
2. Cotton balls
3. Glue
4. Black pens

HOW TO DO IT

1. Discuss with the children how clouds are formed: Water vapor in the air sticks together around little specks in the air. Clouds take on different forms depending on how high they are:
   - *Cirrus clouds* are feathery curls of ice crystals very high in the sky. Sometimes when they are in the sky a storm will follow.
   - *Cumulus clouds* are large, puffy clouds. They look like giant cotton balls in the sky. Sometimes thunderstorms occur when there are lots of these clouds in the sky.
   - *Nimbostratus clouds* are low, dark-gray clouds. They always bring rain.
   - *Stratus clouds* are low clouds that spread across the sky. The weather is usually calm when they are present.
2. Have the children fashion each type of cloud out of cotton and glue it onto a separate sheet of blue paper. Label each cloud.
3. Go outside each day this week to look for clouds. Let the children take turns identifying them and predicting the weather from them.
4. Have some fun with what you've all just learned: Read *The Cloud Book* by Tommy DePaola.

Making Fog

SETTING THE STAGE

Invite the child to make a cloud in a bottle:

You've seen clouds, drawn clouds, and maybe even flown through a cloud in an airplane. Now, how would you like to *make* a cloud?

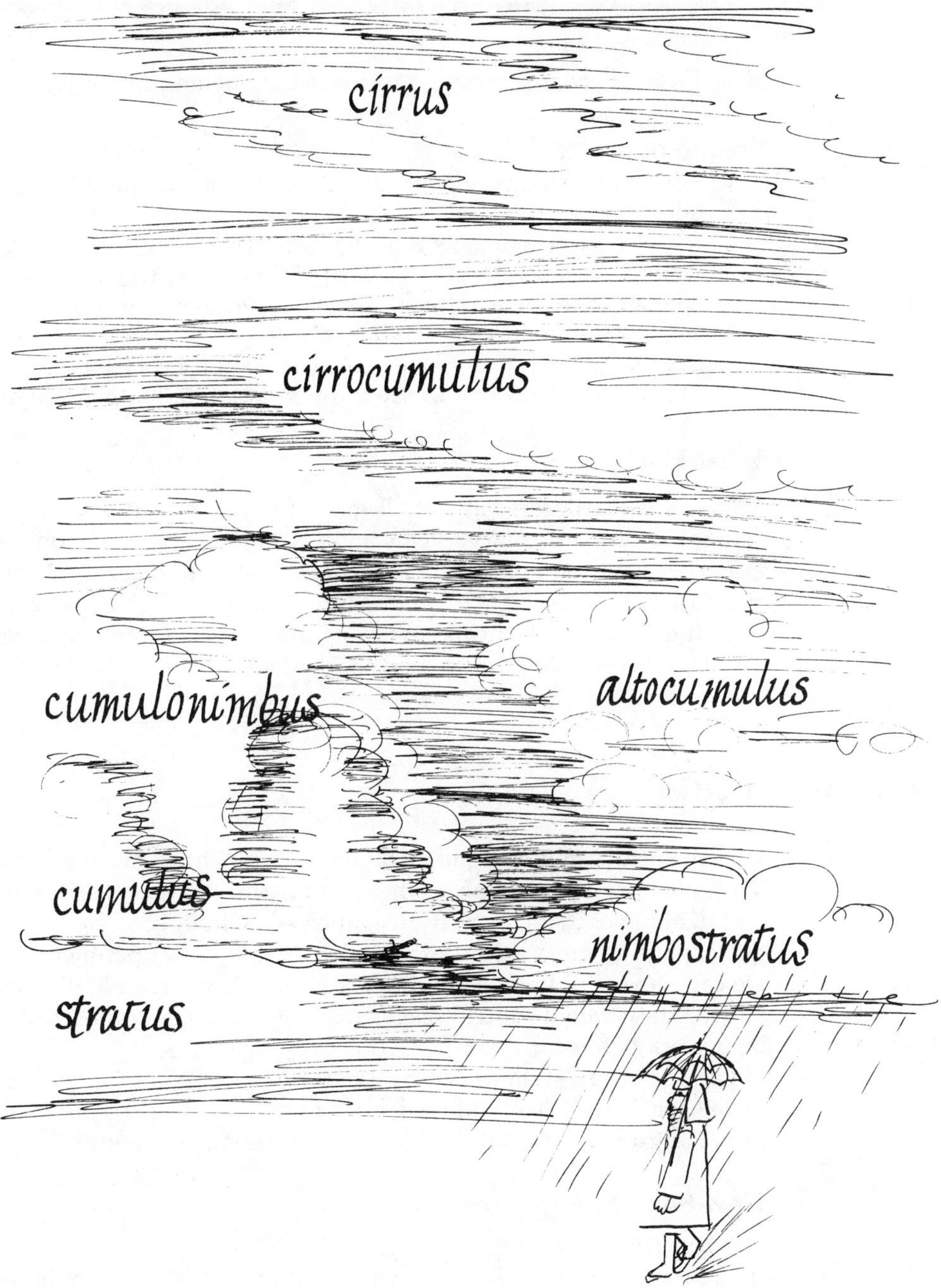

cirrus

cirrocumulus

cumulonimbus

altocumulus

cumulus

nimbostratus

stratus

WHAT YOU'LL NEED

1. Small-mouthed jar or bottle
2. Hot tap water
3. Piece of ice large enough to cover the opening in the jar
4. Cold water

HOW TO DO IT

1. Rinse the jar with hot water and then fill it about one-third full of hot water.
2. Place an ice cube on top of the bottle and have the children watch what happens when the air heated by the hot water meets the cold air from the ice cubes. (When warm, moist air cools down, the moisture condenses and forms drops of water.)
3. Try the same procedure with cold water in place of the hot. Invite the children to watch to see if the same thing happens. Why?

What Else

You and the children can put all this information to use for you by setting up your own weather station. Chart the weather on your calendar. Note wind speed, cloud type, and temperature. Observe trends in the weather and try your hands at forecasting. Each morning, have the children take turns predicting the weather for the day. Write these predictions down, and then check them later on in the day to see how accurate the forecasts were.

LEARNING ABOUT LIGHT

We are surrounded by light—whether it comes from the stars or the lightbulb hanging from the ceiling. Light has become such an intimate part of our lives that we rarely give much extra thought to the essential part it plays in our world. With a little research and experimentation, we can show children something about how it works. What's more, with a little creativity and intelligence, they can discover ways to make light work better for them.

Guided observation will demystify the boundlessness of space and its celestial bodies. The child will learn to cook with light. And finally, the youngsters will even think of new games to play with it.

How Solar Energy Works

SETTING THE STAGE

Invite the children to discover what the sun can do for them besides improve a tan:

If you were asked to describe your favorite kind of weather, you would probably say "a bright, sunny day." A lot of people would agree with you, too. There are so many good things you can do when the sun shines brightly. You can swim, ride your bike, or just go for a walk.

There's something else you can do on a bright, sunny day, too. You can cook! You can do that any day, of course, even at night when the sun isn't shining—unless you want to use the sun instead of the stove to cook with.

There's lots of energy coming to the earth from the sun. With a few special tools, you can use that energy to heat your home and the water you take a bath with. You can bake bread with solar energy and—yes—even make tea!

WHAT YOU'LL NEED
1. Quart jar filled with water
2. 4 teabags

HOW TO DO IT
1. Explain to the children that you are going to use energy from the sun instead of the stove to make tea. The glass jar will gather and trap the heat, which will make the water in the jar steep the tea.
2. Drop the teabags in the jar and put on the lid.
3. Place the jar in direct sunlight for the afternoon.
4. At teatime, serve the sun-tea chilled over ice.

When Up Looks like Down,
and Red Looks Like Green

Invite the child to try out some scientific "magic":

If you loved the color green and wanted to see a picture of a big green balloon, would you get a picture of a red one instead?

Do you think it would be possible to see how it would be if all your friends looked *exactly* the way you do?

And what if you could set the world spinning?

Well, you may not be able to *really* make these things happen, but you can make it *seem* like these things are really happening, by creating *illusions*.

Now, let's try to change the way the world *seems*.

WHAT YOU'LL NEED
1. 2 large mirrors
2. 3 pieces of white paper
3. Red and green crayons
4. Paper
5. Scissors
6. Tape
7. Pen

HOW TO DO IT
1. Explain to the children that they can see a green balloon when all they have is a red one: Color a big red balloon on a piece of paper. Place it in front of the children alongside a plain white piece of paper. Have the children stare at the red balloon for several moments, then quickly look at the plain paper. Ask the children, "Where do you suppose the green balloon came from?" Try this trick with a green balloon and the same piece of plain paper. Ask the children if they can guess what trick their eyes are going to play on them this time. (Here is a simple explanation. The parts of your eye [rods and cones] that see red and green work together. If the ones that see red get tired, the ones that see green take over.)
2. Tell a girl that you're going to invite a roomful of friends in for a while, but not to worry, they will all look just like her. Have the child hold a mirror at arm's length directly in front of her. Hold the other mirror facing the back of her head. Have the child look straight ahead into the mirror. Where did all those good-looking children come from!?
3. Explain to the children that to set the world spinning, they must first set their own bodies whirling. Ask the children to start spinning in place. It will be easy for them to explain why everything else seems to be moving now. When you ask the children to stop, have them look around and tell you what they see—and why.

1.

```
┌──────────────────────────────────────────────────────┐
│ A                                          <----- ½  A │
└──────────────────────────────────────────────────────┘
```

Match A to A - a half twist'

Tape ends together

Draw line down the middle of the strip

Cut along line

2.

```
┌──────────────────────────────────────────────────────┐
│ A                                          <---- ⅓    │
│                                            <----- ⅓  A │
└──────────────────────────────────────────────────────┘
```

Tape as before after matching A to A
Cut into thirds

4. Here's an exercise that's not exactly an illusion, but it will certainly bring the child to wonder exactly what is there and what isn't. Make a *Moebius strip* by cutting a strip of paper about 1 by 8 inches. Hold the strip in front of you with each hand holding one end. Twist *one* end once and then tape the two ends together, keeping the twist in place. With a pen, draw a line down the middle of the strip. Don't lift the pen until you come back to where you started—if you can! Ask the children where the line went.

5. Make another Moebius strip as before and cut it in half lengthwise so you will end up with two thin strips—or will you?

6. Make another Moebius strip, this time cutting it into thirds to make three circles—or is it two?

7. By now, the children (and yourself as well, no doubt) will be wondering what is real and what is just a friendly trick or illusion that you are playing on yourself. The only thing to do is pour some lemonade for all concerned and contemplate! You might want to invite discussion among the children about times when they have seen things that did not appear the way they usually did. How did they decide what was real?

Measuring Shadows

SETTING THE STAGE

Invite the child to use playtime to make some interesting discoveries:

If you wanted to talk to someone down the hall, but you didn't want to get up, you could still communicate by raising your voice a little. But what if your friend in the other room was reading and the lightbulb burned out?

Could you help that person by turning on more lights in *your* room?

You can easily figure out the answer to this, but do you know why this is true?

The reason is just as simple as the answer you just gave. Sound can travel around corners, which is why you can talk to someone who isn't directly in front of you. Light, on the other hand, only moves in a straight line.

If something or someone blocks the straight path of light, the area beyond that point is dark. We call this dark area a *shadow*.

Shadows are lots of fun to play with and they also tell us something about the relationship between the sun and the earth.

WHAT YOU'LL NEED
1. Colored chalk
2. Clock
3. Tagboard
4. Pencil
5. Flashlight

HOW TO DO IT
1. Have the children step outside and find the greatest source of light we know on earth: the sun. Now find an open space on the sidewalk or driveway where the children can do some drawing.
2. Chalk off an 8-by-10-foot area. Write a message to any observers that might stroll by: "Please do not step inside these lines. Scientific experiment in progress."
3. Sometime around midmorning, have one child stand in the center of the test site and have another child trace the first youngster's shadow.
4. Write down the exact time next to the head of the shadow.
5. Have the children color in the shadow. They can use solid coloring or cross-hatching, or they can draw in an actual likeness of the child who cast the shadow.
6. Every hour or two, have the children follow steps 3 to 5. Continue until no more shadows can be cast.
7. Older children will enjoy learning this lesson in the following way: Demonstrate what is happening with the sun and the earth by holding a large sheet of tagboard perpendicular to the ground to represent the earth's surface. Hold a pencil perpendicular to the paper. Have someone else hold a flashlight, representing the sun, in one place while the child with the pencil and tagboard rotates the paper. (Make sure the pencil is always perpendicular to the paper.)
8. Use shadows as an artistic medium to create letters, animals, and anything else you can imagine.

What Else

You can lead the children in further exploration of light during their regular playtime activities: Make a picture book of shadows. Make a sundial in your own backyard. Get a book of M. C. Escher's work and have the children, after being sufficiently awed, put pen to paper and make some optical illusions of their own. And during the next heat wave, the kids may not be able to fry an egg on the sidewalk, but they can explore what kind of cooking they *can* do.

You may enjoy reading *Light, Mirror and Lenses* by F. E. Newing and Richard Bowood. For further information on solar energy, write: National Solar Heating and Cooling Information Center, P.O. Box 1607, Rockville, MD 20850.

HOW TO MAKE DISCOVERIES

Discoveries happen in many different ways. Sometimes they occur quite by "accident," as was the case with the discovery of the law of gravity. People had been watching apples fall from trees for centuries, but one day Isaac Newton saw something new in this age-old phenomenon. Other discoveries, of course, have been made as a result of methodical experimentation.

As children become familiar with various ways to experiment, something special happens. Each experiment serves as an exercise to make a scientific discovery. What's more, it simultaneously increases the child's ability to reason and to logically formulate conclusions. The methodical order inherent in scientific research allows girls and boys to formulate intelligent questions and successfully reach an answer—a worthwhile ability to have even when one is not dabbling in science!

Yes or No

SETTING THE STAGE
Invite the child to begin scientific discovery in an easy and fundamental way:

Making new discoveries can be very exciting. Sometimes you're sure about what you want to learn, but you're not too sure how to go about it.

Well, the first thing you need do is think of exactly what it is you want to know. A good way to start out is to think of a question that can be answered with either a "yes" or a "no." For instance, if you've just found an old magnet in the garage, you might be wondering what to do with it. If there is a nail stuck to it, but the newspaper lying next to it is *not* stuck, the next step might be to find the answer to the question, "Which objects will stick to the magnet?"

Now that you know how to go about it, let's discover some answers!

WHAT YOU'LL NEED

1. A basket containing several small objects, some made of metal and the others made of any other material
2. Magnet
3. 2 labels, one reading "yes," the other reading "no"

HOW TO DO IT

1. Let the children take turns touching the magnet to each object. If the object sticks to the magnet, it should be placed next to the "yes" label. If it doesn't, it belongs with "no."
2. The children have just answered the scientific question, "Will this object be attracted by a magnet?" Ask them if they can make any generalizations based on the information they have discovered.
3. Children have a lot of questions about the whys and hows of the world around them. If you can easily formulate some of these questions into ones that require "yes" or "no" answers (for instance, "Will this object sink when I drop it in a bowl of water?"), you will be providing your beginning scientists with a great format for making discoveries.

Test It Out

SETTING THE STAGE

Invite the children to begin learning in a new scientific way:

Think of all the ways you can use your imagination. It can help you to create things that never existed before, or to look at things that *already* exist in a new and different way.

But how will you know whether or not your new idea will work, or if your new discovery is really true? The answer is simple. You test it out!

Scientists do this all the time. You can do it, too. First you think of something to test out and then you make a list of all the ways you want to test it out.

Here is a way for you to practice this new method of discovering things. Once you know how to use this method, you can test out almost anything you are curious about!

WHAT YOU'LL NEED

1. Tape

HOW TO DO IT

1. Discuss with the children the importance of our thumbs: Humans and primates are the only animals that have them; this fact sets us apart from the other animals, because thumbs allow us to do a great many things. If you don't believe how important our thumbs are to daily activity, let's find out how we would get along without them.

2. Tell the children that the theory you will test out is whether children can perform routine daily activities without their thumbs. Have all the children who want to participate in the experiment hold the thumbs of each hand across their palms. You tape the thumbs in place.

3. Have the children continue on with their regular activity. It is best to include a variety of activities, such as eating, writing, and playing.

4. After an hour or two of this (or as long as the children can last!), bring everyone together and discuss their experiences.

5. You've just introduced the children to an interesting way to answer many of their "what if" questions. They only need to test it out!

Look and See

SETTING THE STAGE

Invite the children to create some changes and then investigate them:

Did you know that you are very powerful individuals? Everything each of you does makes a difference to someone or something else.

Take water, for example. You drink it every day, but did you know you could change water so that you could walk on it? Or change it so that it becomes invisible?

Well, with a few tools you can find in your kitchen, you can do just those very things!

WHAT YOU'LL NEED

1. Pitcher of water
2. Saucepan
3. Ice-cube tray

HOW TO DO IT

1. Explain to the children that you are going to subject water to different temperatures and see what happens to it: Heat to boiling one-third of the water in the saucepan and put one-third in the ice-cube tray in the freezer. Leave the remaining water in the pitcher at room temperature.

2. Check each container periodically and note the condition of the water.

3. When the children *do* notice changes in the form of the water in two of the containers, discuss these changes. Ask the children what they think made the changes occur.
4. Explain to the children that they have just done something to cause a change in something else. They can do any number of things *to* any number of things. Then, just look and see!

What Else

The importance of experimentation goes beyond the obvious elements of an enjoyable new way to learn. These experiments bring the child to a new way of thinking in a clear and productive way, whether he or she is planning a party, writing a letter, or taking a closer look into the backyard. Here are a few suggestions on how to creatively use these new ways of thinking and gaining knowledge.

The youngest scientists in your group can continue experimenting with the "yes" and "no" method, which will answer questions such as "Will this object stay the same if it is left in water overnight?" or "Will this object stay afloat in a bowl of water?"

The more experienced scientist will enjoy exploring the realm of cause and effect in the "Test It Out" set of experiments, in which the child carefully examines all the things that happen as the result of one change. More experiments like this can involve putting a variety of nonliving objects in boiling water and recording the results or freezing a variety of fresh fruits and vegetables and seeing how they've changed, if at all, once they've thawed.

After achieving success with several of these simpler types of experiments, young scientists will join the ranks of professional researchers as they work with classical experimentation using control and experimental groups as in the "Look and See" exercise with water. More fun along this line will reveal the needs of plants (that is, light, air, and water) and what it is you need to make bubbles besides soap and water.

20 DIFFERENT THINGS TO DO ON A NATURE WALK

Everyone loves a walk in the woods. Avid hikers love a challenging trail. Artists and poets translate the natural beauty into pictures and words. Scientists examine changes in plants and animals. The human spirit is revitalized in a special way in fresh natural surroundings.

Children, who seem to have such a lively affinity for nature already, will easily soak up all that the great outdoors has to offer, and will enjoy many nature-oriented projects, such as those outlined in this section. But first, a word or two of caution to your young explorers:

Our first inclination upon leaving a beautiful, natural environment is to take some of it with us. Just one pretty rock or a cutting from a favorite plant, we think, wouldn't be missed. This, of course, is not true, because parks and wildlife preserves are for everyone to enjoy just as they are, and everything contained there is necessary to preserve their ecological balance. There are some things you *can* do to liven up a nature walk, however, and you can even bring things home without disturbing the natural environment. Read on.

SETTING THE STAGE
Invite the children to go for a very special walk:

Think back to the last time you walked through a park or forest. Picture in your mind how very peaceful and beautiful it all was. It looked that way because park rangers check the area every day to make sure everything is in order.

There is another important reason why parks stay so nice: You! You and all of the other people who visit our parks each day must take special care to maintain the environment by leaving it just the way you found it.

But leaving it the way you found it doesn't mean you can't have fun!

WHAT TO DO BEFORE YOU GO
1. Decide on a place to go. Check the types of trails the parks have and, based on this, choose the park that best suits your group.
2. Make sure everyone dresses comfortably, according to the weather. The children should wear long pants or shorts with kneesocks to protect their legs, as well as comfortable walking shoes.
3. Put paper, pencils, crayons, glue, and a few paper bags in your knapsack.
4. Pack a lunch and a thermos of cold water. Stash these in your knapsack, too.

WHAT TO DO WHILE YOU'RE THERE
1. Go on a tactile scavenger hunt. Give each child a list of objects to find. List things by how they feel rather than by name.
2. Collect things that have fallen from trees and bushes. Let the children use them to make a collage when they get home.
3. Invite the children to use the crayons and paper to make leaf and bark rubbings.
4. Go for a blind walk: One child closes his or her eyes, and another child leads the first down a path. The "nonseeing" child should pay special attention to the sounds and feel of things.
5. Have the children collect objects with interesting designs they can use to make tempera or ink prints with when they get

home. (Make sure these objects are not "stolen" from any living things.)

6. Show the children how to weave or braid together some grasses.

7. Walk through a field with no shoes on. Explain to the children that the way you are all collecting burrs and seed pods on your socks is the same way animals collect them in their fur. This is one way that seeds get planted all over fields and forests.

8. Collect fallen objects by categories (for instance, grasses, seed pods, or leaves).

9. Make a glue design on the paper, then sprinkle some sand or soil on it to make a lasting memento.

10. Collect fallen sticks and other attractive objects the group can use to make a mobile later on.

11. Collect some pretty fallen leaves. The children can make a window hanging by ironing them between two pieces of waxed paper. Some crayon shavings sprinkled around the leaves make this craft especially attractive.

12. Have the children look for some animal footprints and make some prints of their own.

13. Pick up litter.

14. Write out directions or draw a map on how to get to a certain place in the park (not too far away). Have the children follow the directions to that place and meet you there.

15. Invite the children to crawl along a path for a while to get an animal's-eye view of the environment.

16. Collect some objects that can be cast in plaster of Paris.

17. Watch out for animals. Sit together at a distance and keep perfectly still. Have the children imagine what it is really like to be an animal.

18. When you are resting or during a walk, play an alphabet game. Each person thinks of things that are visible to the group that begin with each letter in the alphabet (for example, A—acorn, B—burr).

19. Play a guessing game. One person describes something you've all seen on your walk, and everyone else guesses what it is.

20. Make up some poetry as you go along. Remind the children that poetry needn't always rhyme!

WHAT TO DO AFTERWARD

1. Keep the excitement of the day alive by listing all the things you did and saw. Make special note of what you'd like to do again, and of things you didn't do but would like to try next time. Encourage all the children to contribute to the list.

2. Have the children make posters showing how beautiful and enjoyable your natural walk was.

3. Find some willing spot in your yard and plant the burrs, seeds, and so forth that each of you collected on your socks. Water them and watch to see what happens.
4. Have the children dig into their bags of treasures and carry out some of the projects suggested here.

VISITING PLACES WHERE ANIMALS LIVE

Around the time of the Industrial Revolution, zoos sprang up all around the world, not only to entertain, but to serve a purpose for the animal kingdom as well: Most zoos, then as now, actively participate in conservation and propagation programs for rare and endangered species. In addition, larger zoos conduct research in animal medicine, behavior, and disease control.

giraffe

Lion

Zoos have grown in capacity and sophistication over the years and continue to be a delight to children and grownups as well. Children, especially, are fascinated by viewing (and hearing) close-up an animal that they may have only encountered in books. In short, a visit to the zoo is an exciting and enjoyable way for both children and adults to spend a bright, sunny afternoon. The outing is sure to be fun for all concerned, and everyone—even *you*—is sure to learn just a little bit more about our many cohabitants on our planet.

SETTING THE STAGE
Invite the children to discover what a zoo is all about:

Who knows what a *zoo* is? Who knows what another *name* for zoo is?

That name is *zoological gardens*. Now why do you suppose a zoo is called a garden?

collee n's

Elephant

When we think of a garden, we think of a place where we grow plants. But a *zoological* garden is a place where we grow *animals!*

A zoo is a place where animals are kept so that we can enjoy them and learn about them. But a zoo is *also* a place where sick animals are cared for and where animals that have lost their natural home can make a new home so that they can grow and even have babies.

The place where an animal lives in nature is called its *natural habitat.* Zookeepers do their best to make each animal's zoo-house as much like its natural habitat as possible so that the animal will feel at home.

WHAT TO DO BEFORE YOU GO

1. Call your local zoo. Find out the hours it is open, admission charges, when the feeding times are, and if there are any special programs young children might enjoy.
2. Gather as many library books as you can that deal with animals. (You may even stage a pre-zoo field trip to the library.)

183

3. Ask each child to name two favorite animals. Make a list of these animals. Encourage the children not to repeat any animals on the list.

4. Let each child "research" his or her two animals. This information can be about the animals' natural habitats, their eating or sleeping habits, and just plain interesting facts (for example, did you know that the rhino's horn is actually a mass of matted hair?). Have the children record their findings in booklet form.

5. Call the children together and share your research. Note interesting things about each animal that you can look for on your visit to the zoo.

6. Have each child bring a notebook and colored pencils, and be on your way.

WHAT TO DO WHILE YOU'RE THERE

1. Have fun! Spend as long as you like at each exhibit. Enjoy the animals, but do caution the children about teasing and feeding them.

2. Look for special things about each animal. How are the animal's quarters made to resemble its natural habitat? Try to spot some of those interesting characteristics your researchers uncovered. Note how the animals are passing their time—eating, sleeping, bathing, playing?

3. Invite the children to draw pictures of their favorite animals.

4. Be sure to read aloud the informational plaques beside each exhibit. You and the children are sure to discover something new.

5. Talk about what the animals might be thinking when they look at you!

WHAT TO DO AFTERWARD

1. Invite the children to share their impressions about the zoo along with the pictures they drew. Ask each child to name one *new* animal he or she saw and one new fact discovered.

2. Make a chart of animal sizes, from the smallest to the largest.

3. Judging from what you noticed about habitats at the zoo, talk about where you think each animal may have come from, and which ones may have lived together in the wild.

4. Categorize animals by their major characteristics, such as four-legged, winged, or two-legged. Don't forget a category for those animals that look most like humans.

5. Explain the idea of camouflage—an animal's natural protective device—to the children, and show them how it works with this demonstration: Hold a collection of multicolored marbles, buttons, jellybeans, and so on in your palm. Let the children observe how distinct each one is. Now toss them onto a carpet or lawn. Which of the objects stand out? Which ones blend into the background?

A DAYTIME VISIT TO THE NIGHT SKY

People have been fascinated by the sky since the dawn of recorded history. It is filled with luminous, life-giving sunlight by day, which is extinguished at night when the sky becomes a backdrop of infinite black upon which super-radiant beads dance through the night. The wonder we have when we gaze up into the night sky is no doubt akin to the same awesome feeling the first humans had.

It's fun for children to observe changes in the sky and tell stories—fact and fiction—of why and how these changes come about. The entertaining and informative show at the planetarium is a great boost to the lives of both the dedicated amateur astronomer and the child who only occasionally pauses beneath the night sky.

SETTING THE STAGE

Invite the child to see a very special sky show:

> What were you doing last night? Did you stay at home and play indoors or did you go on an outing somewhere?
>
> If you went out to do something at night, no matter how much fun you had, there was something else you could have enjoyed. Even if you stayed at home, you could have enjoyed this.
>
> All you need to do to have some special fun at night is to go outside and look up into the sky. The night sky has fascinated people for a long, long time just as it fascinates people today. For many years, people have studied it and written books about how they thought it came to be.
>
> The best time to look at the night sky is very early in the morning, long before the sun comes up, at about 1:00 or 2:00 A.M. That's much too late (or too early) for you to be up, but guess what? There's a place you can go during the *day* to see the night sky. It's called the *planetarium*.

WHAT TO DO BEFORE YOU GO

1. Find an interesting planetarium show to see. If you don't know where one is, phone your local college or university. Ask for the physical science or astronomy department, and find out if they have a planetarium that is open to the public. If they don't, they will know where one is.

2. Contact the planetarium office for show dates, times, and the subject of the program.

3. If you like, make a brief visit to your local library and read up on the subject of the show. Or if you and the children like surprises, just be on your way!

WHAT TO DO WHILE YOU'RE THERE

1. Buy your tickets.

2. Take a brief stroll around to see the exhibits, look at books, and read any literature the planetarium distributes.

185

3. Line up in plenty of time to get a good seat. (Speaking of this, ask the children why they suppose the seats are built the way they are.)

4. Now, just sit back and enjoy the show!

WHAT TO DO AFTERWARD

1. Have the children make a mural depicting what they've learned.

2. Invite each child to embroider a favorite celestial scene.

3. Research more information on what you learned today. Share this knowledge with the children and encourage them to speculate on the unknown. You may delve into quasars or black holes, or maybe come up with a new myth or two.

4. The children may enjoy making some "astronomy cookies": Use powdered sugar or frosting colored with food coloring to decorate large, plain sugar cookies to resemble a favorite constellation, the markings of a particular planet, or any other member of the heavens.

5. Reinforce and embellish your daytime visit to the night sky in any of the many areas of interest each child has: Cook star cookies and serve them in the shape of a constellation; appliqué or construct a papier mâché model of the solar system; perform an experiment to see the effect pounding rain has on a newly formed planet (a heap of soil will suffice); devise a new theory on the origin of the universe; tell a story about a first trip to Mars . . . The possibilities are as infinite as the universe itself!

6. Go outside on a clear night and try to find what you saw at the Planetarium. Have the children record their observations with silver gummed stars on black paper.

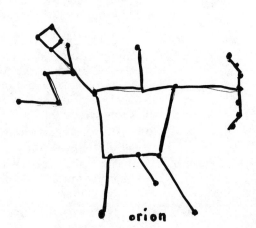

orion

BOOKS FOR CONTINUING DISCOVERY

Books for Adults

ALLISON, LINDA. *The Sierra Club Summer Book.* New York: Sierra Club Books, Charles Scribner's Sons, 1977.

BROWN, VINSON. *The Amateur Naturalist's Handbook.* Englewood Cliffs, N.J.. Prentice-Hall, 1980.

COBB, VICKIE. *Science Experiments You Can Eat.* Philadelphia: Lippincott, 1972.

GERSTENFELD, SHELDON L., DVM. *Taking Care of Your Dog.* Reading, Mass.: 1979.

GOLDSTEIN-JACKSON, KEVIN. *Experiments with Everyday Objects.* Englewood Cliffs, N.J.: Prentice-Hall, 1978.

LINK, MICHAEL. *Outdoor Education.* Englewood Cliffs, N.J.: Prentice-Hall, 1981.

MITCHELL, JOHN. *The Curious Naturalist.* Englewood Cliffs, N.J.: Prentice-Hall, 1980.

NEWING, F.E., and RICHARD BOWOOD. *Light, Mirrors and Lenses.* Loughborough, England: Ladybird Books Ltd., 1962.

NUSSBAUM, HEDDA. *Plants Do Amazing Things.* New York: Random House, 1977.

SIMON, SEYMOUR. *Projects with Plants.* New York: Franklin Watts, Inc., 1973.

SKELSEY, ALICE, and GLORIA HUCKABY. *Growing Up Green.* New York: Workman Publishing, 1973.

Books for Children

ASCH, FRANK. *Turtle Tale.* New York: Dial Press, 1980.

BRANLEY, FRANKLIN. *A Book of Stars for You.* New York: Thomas Y. Crowell, 1967.

BRANLEY, FRANKLIN. *Big Dipper.* New York: Thomas Y. Crowell, 1962.

DEPAOLA, TOMMY. *The Cloud Book.* New York: Scholastic Book Service, 1977.

MAESTRO, GIULIO. *The Remarkable Plant in Apartment 4A.* New York: Bradbury Press, 1973.

REY, H.A. *Find the Constellations.* Boston: Houghton Mifflin, 1976.

CHAPTER EIGHT

SOCIAL GRACES

AN APPLE FROM THE TEACHER

 Social grace, otherwise known as "behaving" or "good manners," is an important part of everyone's upbringing. Our memories of this may vary greatly, depending on our own families' specific codes. Rules may have ranged from "sit down and be quiet" to formal instruction in the proper way to introduce one's best friend to visiting Aunt Martha.

While many social amenities may seem to be primarily for the benefit of adults, there is something very special for the child as well. By learning "proper procedure," children free themselves from the awkwardness and helplessness of not knowing what to do in a given situation, something which inevitably creates wrong behavior or mere passivity. The child who is well versed in the common rules of social grace can handle many situations with ease, however, to the benefit of everyone involved.

For instance, knowing how to use the telephone facilitates a child's ability to communicate with others and is also extremely helpful when adults are too busy to answer the phone. And in an emergency, knowing how to dial the number of a neighbor or the special emergency number may save the child and others from serious injury.

This quantum leap in gaining independence, for that is the essence of social grace, will have only a positive effect on the child's self-confidence. He or she will become more self-sufficient in dealing with others in work *and* play. Social ties will be established and personal relationships will be easily developed within the realm of cultured social grace.

As with the growth of any accomplishments, the development of the basics naturally leads the child to explore the possibility of refining his or her skills. A four-year-old's tea party of crackers and juice, for example, will handily lead to "tea" with homemade punch and cookies at age seven. As this young host or hostess grows in experience and creativity, tea parties will eventually give way to well-organized parties with "official" invitations, decorations, special food, music, and, of course, lots of friends, all of which will be led by a gracious and self-assured host or hostess.

TELEPHONE MANNERS

We feel a sense of pride mixed with a certain sense of loss the first time we hear our child answer the phone with a crisp "Kelley residence, Shannon speaking." That little tyke of ours is most certainly growing up.

Learning to use the telephone is one of the great markers in the child's journey toward independence. From now on, this wonder-kid can talk to whomever he or she pleases, *when*ever he or she pleases. No grownups necessary, thank you very kindly.

Happily, most children wear this newfound freedom well. Once they have been taught the basic rules of telephone etiquette, they almost always treat the telephone with proper respect and dignity. And as they progress in skills directly relating to using the telephone, they grow in others as well: They begin to refine their verbal communication skills. They learn to "make conversation," to make plans, and to deliver messages. Dialing and remembering telephone numbers also improves visual discrimination and auditory memory, two skills necessary for learning to read.

What's more, when a child is able to use the telephone, emergency help is never far away.

Finally, there are some children whose shyness inhibits polite conversation when they are face to face with a new friend or adult. For these youngsters, the visual anonymity afforded by the telephone allows them to "be themselves" and converse freely and fluently.

SETTING THE STAGE

Invite the children to practice some telephone manners:

> Do you ever talk on the telephone? If you do, you know how much fun it can
> be to chat with someone you can't even see. You also know that there are
> certain ways in which you can best use your telephone.

For example, you need to speak *into* the part with lots of holes. You must speak clearly. You mustn't shout. And you should never answer a question by simply shaking your head!

Can you think why?

Using good manners is very important when you use the telephone. It makes telephoning much more pleasant for everyone.

WHAT YOU'LL NEED
1. White paper
2. Black markers
3. Two toy telephones

HOW TO DO IT
1. Demonstrate the proper way to answer the telephone by picking up the receiver of a toy phone and saying "Hello, ———— residence, ———— speaking." Have the children repeat this after you, substituting their names for yours.
2. Write, "Hello, —— residence, ———— speaking" on a sheet of paper. Place it where all the children can see it, then have each child take a turn "answering" the toy phone, using the proper format and substituting his or her name where it is appropriate.
3. Demonstrate how to make a telephone call by dialing a 7-digit number and saying, "Hello, this is ———. May I please speak to James?" Again, have the children repeat this after you.
4. Write the same format on another sheet of paper, place it in front of the children, and have them practice *making* calls. (They can dial numbers from a telephone directory, if you have one available.)
5. Demonstrate the way to get someone else to the telephone by "answering" a toy phone and saying, "Just one moment, please. I'll go get my dad." And then, "My daddy will be right with you."
6. Write *this* format on a sheet of paper and let the children practice answering the toy phone and going to get their "dad."
7. Break the children up into pairs and let them take turns making and receiving phone calls on the toy phones.
8. To give the children practice in dialing, dictate a phone number for each child to dial, then write a phone number down on paper and have each child dial from this.
9. If it is practical, let each child make a *real* call to a parent, friend, or relative right now.

What Else

Children who can write can also be taught to take messages. They must ask the caller's name and the correct spelling, write this down, then carefully write down the digits as the caller relays the telephone number. Simple messages above and beyond a call-back can frequently be remembered by the child and delivered verbally. To implement the message-taking procedure, the children may like to make their own customized message forms, containing "name," "message," and "phone number."

A further step along the route to self-reliance is to let the children make their own telephone directories. Get the smallest-sized spiral notebooks, then let each child list his or her friends' names and copy down their telephone numbers. Youngsters with lots of pals would be wise to alphabetize their lists.

Finally, if your community has a "911" or emergency hot-line number, familiarize the children with the number and how to use it. Write it on a printed label on the telephone for quick and easy use.

TWO FOR TEA

No matter what our individual lifestyles are, all of us entertain friends from time to time. Some of us do it formally, others informally. When we do it well, we make our friends feel both welcome and comfortable. And when that happens, we enjoy ourselves, too.

Why not teach children the art of gracious entertaining at an early age? This exercise in social grace need not be elaborate or, heaven forbid, pretentious. All it should do is awaken in the child an awareness of the comforts of others, so that the young host or hostess can find out, firsthand, that the snack that is shared with a special friend tastes ever so much better than the snack that is eaten alone.

The attention to detail that marks this very first "tea party" will vary from youngster to youngster. Just make sure that the plans belong to the child, and the party will surely be the first of many festive and fun occasions.

SETTING THE STAGE

Invite the children to discover the fun of making plans with someone else in mind:

Do you have a special friend? If you do, you know how good you feel when you are around this lucky person.

Do you ever go to this friend's house to play? I'll bet it makes *you* feel special to be the guest.

Sometimes, though, it's just as much fun to treat someone else as a guest as it is to be the guest yourself. You can see how much fun it is today, in fact, by planning a simple party in your home for your special friend.

WHAT YOU'LL NEED TO PLAN YOUR PARTY
1. Paper
2. Pencil
3. Telephone

HOW TO PLAN YOUR PARTY
1. Decide on the time: morning, lunch, afternoon?
2. Decide on the food. Make sure it's food that the child (and special friend) likes, and that the child will be able to help you prepare it. Olive-and-cheese kabobs, hard-boiled eggs, fruit, cookies, or punch are easily manageable possibilities. Make a list of anything you may need to buy.
3. Decide on a theme, if desired. For example, it might be a "teddy bear's picnic," or a bicycle parade, or a tea party to share with favorite dolls. If there are any decorations such as balloons or flowers that would help the theme along, add these to your list, too.

4. When you and the child have decided on the theme, let the child telephone the special friend. A simply written list with all the pertinent information on it will help the child get the invitation straight.
5. If the party is a "go," proceed to phase 2!

HOW TO GIVE THE PARTY
1. Buy whatever is needed.
2. Invite the child to prepare the food. Provide assistance if asked.
3. Let the child set the table or lay the picnic cloth, and put up the decorations.
4. Have the child wash and change into "party" clothes.
5. Remind the child to treat his or her friend as an honored guest.
6. Enjoy!

What Else

Be sure your child helps you clean up when the party is over. This, too, is a part of gracious entertaining!

Other ways to reinforce your child's newfound sensitivity to the comforts of others is to include the youngster in your adult parties occasionally. If you have invited another couple with children to your house for a dinner party, for example, have them bring their children and let your child work on the "mini-party" plans.

Let the child in on preparations, too, such as cooking, decorations, or table settings. Bring up details that will necessarily make the child think of others' comfort, such as, "Uncle Louie is left-handed. Where should we set his place?" Or, "Grandpa doesn't like rice. Should we bake him a potato?" Or, "How about a separate table for the children?"

Finally, share *May I Bring a Friend?* by Beatrice Schenk De Regniers with the young host or hostess.

WHAT DO YOU NEED TO SPEND THE NIGHT?

What a wondrous event it is the first time a child ventures into another home for the night. Any apprehensions or sighs of sadness are almost always on the part of the parent. The child, especially if he or she has been prepared for the event, trots off excitedly and assuredly, with scarcely a backward glance.

The following activity gets the child ready for this monumental event by focusing on the practicalities involved. In addition to gearing up emotionally, the youngster will exercise his or her ability to plan ahead and to separate essentials from nonessentials. (How many adults do you know who always overpack or underpack for any excursion?) The activity is done in such a way as to sharpen the child's memory skills and to give him or her some plain old packing know-how.

Finally, knowing exactly what is necessary for daily care and how to gather these items together gives the child a feeling of self-sufficiency, an attribute that not only carries over into other areas of the youngster's life, but also makes that first night out a pleasurable and comfortable experience.

So much for the child. Now, back to the parent. Do remember that when a child cheerfully goes off for a whole night without missing you, it does not mean he or she loves mom or dad any the less. Quite the contrary. It means that the youngster is secure in the special love that is shared by parent and child.

SETTING THE STAGE

Invite the child to look upon spending the night away from home as a positive adventure;

> Spending the night away from home can be a really exciting adventure. You might spend the night at a friend's house. Or it may be a relative's house. But no matter which place you spend the night, even though you don't know exactly *what* will happen, you can be sure that lots of fun awaits you.
>
> When you sleep over at a friend's house, there are things that will be different from sleeping at your own house: the room and bed, of course, and the mom or dad who tucks you in. You may even eat different foods for breakfast.
>
> But there are things that will be the same, too. Some of them are the things that you bring with you—specific items of your own that you will need and that help you feel at home.
>
> These are the things you need to spend the night!

WHAT YOU'LL NEED

1. A big carton containing: toothbrush, toothpaste, hairbrush, pajamas, underwear, playclothes, and "extras" such as a special book, doll, blanket, or toy, plus hair ribbons, belts, or shoes. (These things can be child-sized, or they can be yours—just so long as each item is easily recognizable.)
2. Suitcase or dufflebag.
3. Paper.
4. Pencils.

HOW TO DO IT

1. For the "dry run," ask the children to take turns naming the things they would need to spend the night. As each item is named, take it out of the carton and "pack" it. Try to *gently* discourage silly or irrelevant guesses.

2. As each item is packed, have each child write it down on a sheet of paper in words or pictures.

3. When the suitcase is all packed and the children's packing lists are complete, return the contents of the bag back to the carton. Let the children take turns packing the suitcase by referring to the list and checking off each item as it has been packed. (If you can dig up two of everything, you can turn this exercise into a fun relay!)

4. When all the children have had a turn, play this guessing game: Place some, but not all, of the items in the bag. Let the children guess which items are missing. The child who correctly names all the missing items can then be the one to partially pack the bag.

What Else

Wrap up the activity by talking about overnight experiences that the children may be planning. What things may happen that will be different from the normal routine? Without dwelling on them, try to draw out any apprehensions the children may have.

You might want to make some "what if" books about spending the night at various places, such as Mars or the North Pole. You may also want to read to the children *The Visit* by Joan Esley. This book suggests the surprises that await the child who is open to new experiences.

Finally, do spend some time on overnight manners: "please" and "thank you," of course; obeying the rules of the new household; eating the food that is served; and cleaning up after oneself. You might also suggest that the child follow up the visit with a "thank you" note, card, or phone call.

THANK YOU VERY MUCH

It is never too early to learn the importance of saying "thank you"! It is one of the best ways we know to let others know how much we appreciate what they have done for us.

Children are taught to say "thank you" as an immediate response to the gratification of some desire. Just about any child will remember to say "thank you" for a cookie or a glass of juice. Yet how many remember to give the thanks that are due after an enjoyable time at a friend's house or after receiving an extra-special birthday gift? Somehow, good manners demand more than just those two words. A special note or other gesture of thoughtfulness eloquently lets Aunt Marian know how extra-happy she has made the child.

Now is the time to teach the child the importance of "thank you" notes. This is one way the children can let their best friends or their favorite uncles know how grateful they are. The notes don't have to be elaborate; especially with these first notes, it is truly the thought that counts. Leave the contents of the note up to the child. You'll be pleasantly surprised at what results from the happy combination of youthful thoughtfulness and creativity. You'll also be delighted at what satisfaction creating the note gives your child.

SETTING THE STAGE

Invite the child to discover another way of saying "thank you":

Has anyone ever done anything really special for you? Like taking you to the beach on a very hot day, or inviting you to a special picnic?

Or have you ever received a birthday or Christmas gift that was *exactly* what you'd always wanted?

Somehow, just saying "thank you" wasn't enough to let your friend know just how much you loved the picnic or how much you enjoy that gift, was it?

When you want to thank people for something *really* special, it's nice to write a "thank you" note to tell them so. This is one way of letting these special people know how much you appreciate their thoughtfulness. And when they know how happy it made you, it makes them happy, too.

So happy, in fact, that they may want to do something nice for you all over again!

WHAT YOU'LL NEED
1. Paper
2. Pens, crayons, colored pencils, markers
3. Stickers
4. Pictures cut from magazines

197

5. Paste
6. Envelope
7. Stamp

HOW TO DO IT

1. Give the child free rein in creating the "thank you" note. It can be all words, or simply an original illustration with "thank you" written across the top. Or it can be a combination of a few words of thanks with original artwork, stickers, or appropriate cut-outs.

2. Make sure the note says "thank you" somewhere, and that it is signed by the child. Other things the note might include are a salutation, a direct reference to the gift or outing, and a sentence or two saying how much the child liked it.

Dear Colleen Kelley i LiKe You alot. Thank You for The Kite From Shannon.

3. Put the note in an envelope. Draw lines in appropriate places for the address and return address. Help the child with the addresses by writing them down on a piece of paper and having the youngster copy them onto the envelope.
4. Place a stamp on the envelope and mail it.

What Else

Help your child think of the occasions when "thank you" notes are called for. When the child does determine that a note would be appropriate, encourage him or her to follow through immediately. It's a thoughtful habit that your child will keep for a lifetime, not to mention one that will delight his or her friends and relatives.

Children who write many notes may like to design some stationery to have on hand. This can be done by making a pretty, colorful border on any 8½-by-11-inch sheet of paper and repeating the border on the edge of a plain white envelope.

Another element of "giving thanks" might be for the children to learn how to say "thank you" in several different languages.

Finally, children that can master the art of a simple thank-you note might be encouraged to try other forms of correspondence—postcards, letters to distant relatives, etc. One way to spark this interest might be a field trip to the local post office.

A PICNIC CAN BE ANYWHERE

If you're looking for a way to make any day extra-special, a picnic is an excellent solution. A picnic *can* be anywhere, for it's not so much the locale that pleases the children, but the idea of a picnic itself. With that in mind, you can have your picnic anywhere from the backyard to the back bedroom to a clearing in a nearby wood, and the kids are sure to be delighted.

This casual approach to mealtime gives the children one more experience to add to their repertoire of social graces. What type of foods, for example, would travel well? How should they be eaten? What extras would make the picnic especially comfortable for those in attendance? A picnic blanket? Pillows? A fly swatter?

Needless to say, planning and preparing for the picnic are half the fun. They also provide an excellent opportunity for the child to practice some logical and creative thinking.

SETTING THE STAGE

Invite the boys and girls to plan the perfect picnic:

Have you ever had a picnic lunch? What's the difference between a picnic lunch and your regular lunch?

One difference is that the food for your picnic is taken someplace other than your regular eating table, and you often eat it outside or on the ground.

That means that you must take special foods: foods that won't melt if it's hot, for example; foods that are easy to carry; and foods that are easy to eat.

Would you take popsicles on a picnic on a hot day? Or hot grilled cheese sandwiches on a cold day? How about a whole chocolate layer cake? It would be good to eat, but could you carry it in a backpack?

So you see, to plan a picnic, you really have to use your head. What would *you* like to bring along?

WHAT TO DO BEFORE YOU GO
1. Assess the weather, and decide on a locale. (Even if it is raining, don't despair! Be creative and rig up an indoor picnic ground somewhere in the house. The kids will love it. To prepare, you might read *Winter Picnic* by Robert Welber.)
2. Discuss the menu. Make sure the food and drinks fit the requirements for picnic food, that you have the ingredients on hand, and that any preparations are simple enough for the children to carry out. (Let as much of the menu as possible be the children's idea.)
3. Discuss ways to keep each food or drink hot, cold, or fresh.
4. Make a list of everything else you might need to be comfortable, to eat and drink easily, and to clean up. Examples might be pillows, straws, or premoistened towelettes. Remember to keep bring-alongs to a minimum.
5. Divide the children into two teams. One team prepares the food, the other team gathers the other items and does the packing.
6. Let the children decide if there's room to bring a ball, jumprope, or art supplies along.

WHAT TO DO WHILE YOU'RE THERE
1. Find a shady, dry, flat spot on which to set up the picnic.
2. Divide the children into teams again: One lays out the cloth, utensils, and so forth, and the other sets out the food.
3. Enjoy!
4. After lunch, explore the surrounding area, play with equipment you may have brought, or simply lean back and relax.
5. Clean up and pack up. Remember to leave your picnic site as unspoiled as it was when you got there.

WHAT TO DO AFTERWARD
1. This is a good idea for the ride—or walk—home: Play "20 Questions" with the category "Things you can bring on a picnic."
2. Make a "Picnic Cookbook" with ideas for menus for other days. Encourage each child to contribute at least one recipe or idea.
3. Make a group poster or mural that pictorially outlines the sequence of events in preparing for and enjoying a picnic.

Probably the main reason we hesitate to take small children out to eat is that we fear they won't behave and will make us, and others in the near vicinity, uncomfortable. Though the fear is a valid one, it creates a "catch 22" type of situation:

How will children ever learn the proper way to conduct themselves in a restaurant if they never get the opportunity to try?

The answer, of course, is to start small and work up. Given a little practice, the children will soon be able to make knowledgeable decisions from the menu, will patiently await the service from the waitpersons, and will stay seated—except for an occasional trip to the restroom—until the meal is over.

The benefits for both you and your child will be well worth any problems you may have undergone along the way: The children will feel good about themselves when they are included on grownup outings like these and will grow in social presence. And you will find that the freedom to spontaneously choose to eat a meal out, without having to make other arrangements for your child, not only simplifies your

life, but also makes extended stays away from home both feasible and pleasurable for the whole family.

SETTING THE STAGE

Invite the children to ponder the fun and the responsibilities of going "out to eat":

> Eating supper at a real restaurant is certainly different from eating supper at home, isn't it? You sit at a special table in a room with lots of other tables in it. You must sit quietly at your place and be on your best behavior so that you won't disturb the people at the other tables. As a reward, you get to choose *whatever* you want to eat, and you don't even have to clear your place when you're done.

> One of the best things about eating in a restaurant is that it is a grownup thing to do. So if you have been included in a trip to a restaurant, you know that you must be someone special.

WHAT TO DO BEFORE YOU GO

1. Investigate the dining possibilities near your home: Look for a coffee shop or family-style restaurant that offers some sort of formality but also welcomes children.
2. Look into the possibility of taking public transportation to add another dimension to your outing.
3. Plan on arriving at a quiet time—for a very early or very late lunch or a very early dinner.
4. Review restaurant rules of etiquette, such as sitting still, speaking in low voices, keeping hands to selves, and saying "please" and "thank you" to the waitpersons. After emphasizing these "do's," you might want to read *Lily at the Table* by Linda Heller to illustrate the "don't's"!
5. Make sure the children are hungry enough to eat the meals you will be paying for, but not so ravenous that they will be impatient.
6. Dress the children in their best, send them to the bathroom for one last trip, stick some paper and crayons or a small storybook in your pocket, and be on your way.

WHAT TO DO WHILE YOU'RE THERE

1. Point out the bathroom to the children on the way to your table to avoid problems later on.
2. When you are settled in your seats, read the menu to the children. To guarantee good choices, suggest several items from which each child can choose, based on individual taste.
3. Let each child order his or her own meal when the time comes.
4. Pass the time while you wait by discussing the differences between the restaurant and home, talking about what the meal might be like, playing "I spy with my little eye . . .," and, if necessary, passing out paper and crayons or reading a story.

5. When the food comes, remind the children to use good table manners as they eat (use proper utensils, don't play with your food, eat slowly, don't talk with your mouth full).

6. After the meal has been cleared away, spend at least a few minutes just sitting and talking. This is a relaxing and fun way to complete your special meal.

WHAT TO DO AFTERWARD

1. Discuss all the good things about dining out. Let each child tell what he or she likes best about the experience.

2. Try to figure out how you might make one of the favorite foods that was served.

3. If you have a large enough group, set up a restaurant game at a future snack time: Let the children compose the menu (based on what's on hand), set the table, then take turns being waitperson, cook, and diner. (If this occurs after the group has played "The Bank Game," add a mathematical dimension to the activity by providing play money to pay for the food.)

BOOKS FOR CONTINUING DISCOVERY

Books for Adults

GINOTT, DR. HAIM G. *Between Parent and Child.* New York: Avon Books, 1965.

MONTESSORI, MARIA. *The Child in the Family.* New York: Avon Books, 1970.

Books for Children

DE REGNIERS, BEATRICE SCHENK. *May I Bring a Friend?* New York: Atheneum, 1964.

ESLEY, JOAN. *The Visit.* Skokie, IL.: Rand McNally, 1980.

HELLER, LINDA. *Lily at the Table.* New York: Macmillan, 1979.

WELBER, ROBERT. *Winter Picnic.* New York: Pantheon, 1970.

INDEX